BEACHY

The 22p stamp in the series "Safety at Sea"
issued 18 June 1985 shows the lighthouse

John Surtees

S.B. Publications

By the same author
The House Physician's Handbook
Barracks, workhouse and hospital, St Mary's Eastbourne
The Princess Alice and other Eastbourne hospitals
St Wilfrid's, the Eastbourne and district hospice
Chaseley, a Home from Home

First published in 1997 by SB Publications
c/o 19 Grove Road, Seaford, East Sussex BN25 1TP

ISBN   1 85770 118 6

Printed by Island Press Ltd
3 Cradle Hill Industrial Estate, Seaford, East Sussex BN25 3JE
Tel 01323 490222

CONTENTS

The majesty of Beachy Head, Sussex, with man intruding as usual

1   BEACHY HEAD
FROM HOLYWELL TO BIRLING GAP

Choose ye your need from Thames to Tweed,
And I will choose instead
Such lands as lie 'twixt Rake and Rye,
Black Down and Beachy Head.

Sussex   Rudyard Kipling

Beachy Head is the boldest, highest, most romantic and dangerous chalk headland on the south coast of England. Three miles west of Eastbourne, it is the eastern end of the South Downs. The summit of 165 metres (535 feet) above sea level provides glorious views, eastward to Eastbourne and beyond to Pevensey and Hastings; westward to Belle Tout, the Seven Sisters and in the distance Seaford Head, Brighton and Worthing. On an exceptionally clear day Dungeness may be seen to the east and, it is said, the Isle of Wight in the other direction.

The name appears as Beuchef in 1274, was Beaucheif in 1317, becoming consistently Beachy Head by 1724, and has nothing to do with beach, but is a tautological corruption of the original French words meaning Beautiful Headland.

The Head is renowned all over the world and the view sells many a postcard. As HJ Massingham wrote, "Although Wiltshire has three times the chalk of Sussex, it is Sussex Downs which have the reputation."[1]

Eastbourne postal frankings of 1968, proclaiming the town as the "Sun Trap of the South", included two outlines of the Head and the lighthouse, and for a 1985 postage stamp issue "Safety at Sea" the lighthouse was featured on the 22p stamp. Beachy Head was the name of an Atlantic class steam locomotive No. 32424 built in 1911 and destroyed in 1958; not to mention a six-year-old horse in the First National Bank Gold Cup Chase at Ascot in November 1994.* It is found in the expression, "Birmingham by way of Beachy Head", meaning a roundabout way, and it might be argued that the highest accolade of all was inclusion in the 1936 Senior Service cigarette card second series, No. 26, "Sights of Britain".

For our purposes the term "Beachy Head" will be applied to a length of coastal cliffs on the English south coast extending from Holywell (at the western end of the Eastbourne sea front) to Birling Gap, a distance of some four miles (6.4 km).

This definition of "Beachy Head" delineates a bulge of the coastline, clearly demarcated on a map and plain to an observer on the spot, with the lighthouse almost in the middle. You can walk down to the sea at Holywell, from where the 20m (50 feet) high cliffs start to rise to the maximum height of 165m - at a quarter of a mile east of the lighthouse - only to drop down again to about 20m at Birling Gap where there is easy access once more to the beach, by means of a set of temporary steps.

*It came in third, at 3-1.

Most of the chalk cliffs have a sheer vertical face with a thin overhang of soil at the top, but along the eastern half of "Beachy Head" the cliff face can be broken by grassy slopes and ledges.

The Eastbourne promenade rises westwards from near sea level at the pier to form two or three terraces - or parades - of walkways, their slopes planted with hypericum, tamarisk and senecio. It ends at what is now called Holywell, originally the Gore Chalk Pit, and laid out as gardens in 1905 at a cost of £400 - which the Corporation had to borrow. Eastbourne's first municipal motor bus service ran here in 1903 with the destination board reading, "To Foot of Beachy Head". Before 1914 char-à-banc fares from Eastbourne to the top of Beachy Head were 1/6d (7^1/$_2$p), and the cab fare, with a 15 minute stop, was 6 shillings (30p).

All along the promenade paths run down to the beach and below the Italian Gardens, constructed to provide work for the local unemployed in 1922, there is a line of chalets at the edge of the shore. Chalet No. 2 was used by King George V and Queen Mary in March 1935 when staying at nearby Compton Place.

At the far west of the seafront is St Bede's School which recently bought the next door house, almost the last before the cliffs. This is *Holywell Mount* rebuilt for Jack Hullett in 1938. It was the second Mrs Hullett's suicide (she had "threatened Beachy Head," but took an overdose) which sparked off the investigations leading to the arraignment of Dr John Bodkin Adams in December 1956 on a charge of murdering Mrs Edith Morrell, one of his patients.

The first hump of grassland after the parades, the eastern extremity of the South Downs, opens up a view over the Eastbourne front, notable for its absence of shops - thanks to the patronage of the Dukes of Devonshire. Standing out in the middle distance is Eastbourne's 1000-foot long, 60-foot wide pier; and you can imagine the colours of the nearby Carpet Gardens. The pier was a long time in the completion, and opened in 1870 only for a great storm to wash away the shore end in 1877. It shows the effect to this day because you can see the replaced section was built at a higher level than the remaining sea end.

On the left, almost obscured by South Cliff, along King Edward's Parade, is the white sprawl of the Grand Hotel, built in 1877 and famous for the BBC broadcasts by its "Palm Court" Orchestra, starting under Albert Sandler in 1924 and continuing into the 1930s.[2]

From our viewpoint, the Wish Tower (known to holidaymakers as diverse as Charles Darwin and Lewis Carroll) and the Western Lawns are clearly visible. Nearer on the left is Meads, one of the hamlets that went to form Eastbourne. It has an old convalescent hospital, All Saints, with a listed chapel worth a visit.

The Wish Tower was number 73 of the south coast Martello Towers built from 1805 to 1812 to defend the coast against the French.[3, 4, 5] Some say the original name comes from "Martel", old French for a war-hammer, but more probably it is a corruption of "Mortella", the site of a fort in Corsica captured in 1794 by the Royal Navy with some difficulty. The present name is from the marshy land (or "Wish") which used to surround it. That in 1880 it was said to be "almost useless for defensive purposes" didn't stop it being fronted with 6-inch guns in 1940. It was in greater danger of being knocked down after the war, until in 1959 it was given Ancient Monument status and opened as a museum in 1970.

On the Western Lawns the Edwardian ladies paraded in their finery after Sunday church. This was to show they could afford to keep staff at home cooking the lunch, and for their daughters to attract the eye of a beau.

At the end of the prom, Duke's Drive turns inland and as Upper Duke's Drive (B2103) rises by a series of acute bends to join the Beachy Head Road, three-quarters of a mile inland. This leads to the A259, but if you take the first left, signposted, "Beachy Head" and "Birling Gap 4", this runs along the top of the Downs past the Beachy Head Hotel, on to Belle Tout and Birling Gap before joining the A259 at East Dean. Just past the hotel, before the lighthouse, the road veers to within 100m of some of the highest cliffs. To the Eastbourne side of the hotel the road has large pay-and-display car parks on the land side, and past the hotel there are car parks on both sides.

In these parts "Downs" is a term for rounded, turf-covered, chalk hills. Mark Antony Lower says the word comes from the Anglo-Saxon "Dun" meaning a hill.[6] The valleys are called "Bottom", "Coomb" or "Dean".

Holywell

For the walker there are a number of paths westwards. The beach is strewn with large boulders - not making for rapid walking where it is important to know the time of the tides, or there is a path through Meads, or a track along the cliff top. This path begins as Foyle's Way, named after Gilbert Foyle of the London bookshop, who presented land in the area to the town. Iron railings run along the seaward side of the path. The real Holywell is in the next hollow on the way towards the Beachy Head promontory. As Baxter wrote, "half-a-mile from Seahouses [the old name for Eastbourne near the pier] is a chalybeate spring, called Holy-well", and Parry mentions, "...chalybeate spring at Holywell".[7]

In the early 19th century there was a little colony of fisher folk here, their main livelihood was in crabs and lobsters, with some shrimping and prawning - in the days when scallops were 3d a dozen and thought a low class fish.

For the fishermen the well was a source of potable water: its origin explained by the structure of chalk cliffs. Chalk hills stand out because chalk is slightly harder than clay, and it is porous. Surface water rounds off chalk, producing the "blunt, bow-headed whale-backed" appearance (although Massingham compares their shape to reflected cumulus clouds), but as water easily percolates through the chalk it is not worn away so rapidly as less porous rock and dries rapidly after rain. Beneath the chalk lies impervious gault clay and greensand (on which the Wish Tower stands) and these layers hold up the water so that it runs horizontally to emerge at the base, or the side (the scarp), of the Downs as streams and springs. Hence the springs of Holywell which were held in high repute for purity,[8] rather than medicinal properties, and hence the fishermen were moved out to the east when an improved water supply was needed for the town's increasing population and the Eastbourne Waterworks Company installed a pumping station.

In the 1950s there was still a ledge along the Holywell cliffs with a couple of cottages. Leslie Hore-Belisha, of Beacon fame, had one before 1939.

View from Foyle Way east to Pinnacle Point, Eastbourne pier in the distance

Experts tell us chalk is formed under water (sedimentary rock: not strange when you consider Mount Everest was formed under the sea) from the remains of billions of tiny marine algae. When they died their skeletal parts - Coccoliths - sank to the sea floor to form a chalky ooze at a rate of 1mm per 75 years. You may wish to calculate how long it would take to build up the 165000mm of Beachy Head. Crystals of iron pyrites can also be found in the chalk, along with impressions of Brachiopods, Ammonites and Echinoids (sea urchins).

The rows of flint in the chalk were formed from silica in the burrows of marine worms, or from sponges. Sussex is rich in flint, used as weapons and tools by Stone Age man, although Wilmington is the nearest principal flint mine.[9] Flints were mined because dug flints flaked better than flints found on the surface (field flints). On the Downland above Beachy Head flint artefacts have been found from the Palaeolithic and Mesolithic periods, over 15 000 years ago.

The cliffs are sheer because chalk has vertical joints and when the sea undercuts it to expose a joint the whole top section falls. The fallen rocks protect the base of the next section for many years (see Chapter 9).

West from Holywell the first cliffs reach hardly 45m in height and are clothed in bushes and brambles with, in season, the reddish hues of valerian, sea poppies and mallows. There are a few exceptions such as Pinnacle Point (or the Sugarloaf), a sharp pointed cone of white chalk standing out on the beach like a faceted space rocket, although rather worn away these days. Even these cliffs can be dangerous and in September 1967 a blasting operation to remove 1000 tons of chalk was needed to stabilise the cliffs between Pinnacle Point and Holywell.

Whitbread Hollow

The path opens up with a seat and a view back to Eastbourne pier. A little further to the west, about a quarter of the way from Holywell to the lighthouse, is Whitbread Hollow (or White Bread Hole), donated to the Eastbourne Borough Council in the 1920s. The flattish central area has been used as allotments, and as a school sports ground, which had a sports pavilion until it was destroyed by arsonists some years ago. There are pleasant, shaded walks around the sloping landward side, where the ground rises towards the top of the Downs.

Whitbread Hollow, playing fields to the right and cliffs on the left

The militia camped here before 1914, and in 1915 a tented RAMC camp was set up before more permanent buildings were constructed nearer the town at Summerdown Camp. It was mainly for medical staff, for any wounded soldiers would need all the strength imparted by their convalescence to survive a winter on such an exposed spot edged with cliffs, lovely though it is in the summer. These

9

boundary cliffs average about 35m (120 feet) in height, and range from 30m to almost 75 metres.

Other wartime associations abound and unexploded shells are uncovered years afterwards. On 13 April 1975 a section of the Downs overlooking Whitbread Hollow was fenced off after a phosphorus bomb had been exploded by an Army bomb disposal squad. Otherwise this is a delightful part of the Eastbourne area.

The cliff edge is always dangerous. On 18 May 1973 two students sat talking on the edge and one stretched forward to prise a fossil out of the chalk. She felt herself slipping, her 19-year-old companion tried to grab her, and they both fell 35m. The fossil-hunter was killed, but the other student sustained only minor injuries probably because her fall was broken by landing on her colleague.

Cow Gap

A quarter of a mile west of the bowl of Whitbread Hollow the sea cliffs in places drop down to nothing more than grass-covered chalk dunes. At Cow Gap it is possible to walk over chalky white rocks to the shingle beach. It was popular with smugglers. In 1960, after exceptionally heavy rains, there were enormous cliff falls east of the lighthouse and subsidence here has produced broken cliffs with step-like indentations as high as ten metres in places. The main cliffs, covered with gorse and vegetation, are set back some 400m from the shore.

The remains of concrete from 1939-45 gun emplacements can still be seen. On 23 January 1943 a Bofors gun at Cow Gap shot down a German FW190 fighter/bomber which had dropped bombs on Polegate and raked the town with gunfire, killing two women and a soldier on leave. The plane fell into the sea. The Gap looks innocent enough, but in 1843 the *Unione,* an Italian brig laden with fruit and wine, was stranded here and went to pieces, only four of the crew escaping, and on 26 April 1955 a Greek ship, the *Germania,* came ashore after a collision. This time the lifeboat saved the crew and the ship was later towed off.

The sea cliffs rise steadily west of Cow Gap to join up with the main cliffs. Over the length of Coney Bottom they increase rapidly in height from 60m to 125m, but in parts the cliff face is broken by a gentle slope half way down.

Falling Sands

At about 1000m east of the lighthouse the angle of the combined cliffs turns to face south and form a feature known as Falling Sands. This extends to within 550m of the lighthouse and over this stretch the height of the cliffs increases sharply. Jutting out from the bottom of the cliffs at Falling Sands there is 200m of shingle beach. The reason for the descriptive name becomes clear if you are on the beach early in the morning of a windless day when you will hear the soft rustling sound as millions of tiny chalk grains fall down the cliff face, which is most unstable, although some say the Falling Sands were a quicksand bed.

Coming to within half-a-mile of the lighthouse the pathways turn into tracks etched into the grass as they run up the slopes to meet up at the top of the Downs. The Beachy Head road is still well away from the cliff edge and separated by brushwood and irregular ground. Walkers who turn right to cross the road at this point might notice shallow overgrown pools, near Black Robin Farm, and just before the first Beachy Head car park. They are "Dew Ponds" which served the Downs shepherds for the watering of their flocks on the permeable chalk. It is surprising how often they retain water in times of drought (see Appendix 1).

The farms on the land side of the road are Bullock Down and Black Robin. At Bullock Down excavations by the Sussex Archaeological Society have discovered a Neolithic site,[10] and hoards of Roman coins have been found at both places.

The Gorringe family have farmed round here since 1693. Joseph was the farmer at Bullock Down Farm in the 19th century, when part of Sprays Farm.

A 1920s aerial view looking east with (right) lighthouse and (top) pier {S Benz}

The farms are tenanted and for many years grew wheat and barley, with dairy, sheep and pig farming under certain controls, mainly designed to avoid fertiliser contamination of the water supply, because the Downs act as a water gathering zone. Since 1990 the Eastbourne Council has promoted the grazing of sheep, with improved access for the public. The Downs had sheep and shepherds for hundreds of years and they helped to produce the typical Downland turf. Eastbourne Corporation even ran their own flock of sheep at Beachy Head from 1928 to 1950.

Standing on the cliffs, on a fine sunny day, the walker will often observe one of the Eastbourne pleasure boats, such as the *Southern Queen* or *William Allchorn,* on a trip to Beachy Head and the lighthouse. These trips started in 1861.

At 800m from the lighthouse the cliffs are reaching 135m in height with the top 60m sheer, followed by a gentle incline and then a sheer drop again. A further 200m west the first really vertical south-facing sea cliffs cut into the Downs.

The point where Falling Sands ends, some 500m east of the lighthouse, could be taken as the nearest point on the cliffs to the Beachy Head Hotel, although a straight line drawn south west from the hotel to the lighthouse crosses the cliff top 300m east of the lighthouse.

Beachy Head Hotel

An inn nestling just behind the peak of the Downs, has been in existence for well over a century. Originally called the Queen's (from the Marine Parade hotel), it was licensed to stay open an extra hour on Sunday mornings between 1880 and 1967 to cope with the great number of visitors about noon.

Rupert Brooke (1887-1915), the poet who wrote, *Stands the church clock at ten to three? And is there honey still for tea?* and *...there is some corner of a foreign field That is for ever England,* stayed at the Beachy Head Hotel in 1911.

An incendiary bomb dropped in on 25 August 1940, but although there were several bombs on Beachy Head during the war and the Downs were hit by V1s, the hotel escaped. In the aftermath, according to local resident, Dr Paula Gosling, the hotel was little more than a collection of shacks, where the fare was, 'An unending supply of mince followed by bread and butter pudding, with no choice, of course. It was bad enough to put anyone off both bread and butter for life.'

Having survived the war, the Beachy Head Hotel burnt down on 6 April 1966. The fire started about 0600h. Mr Albert Green, one of the fire-fighters at the time said, 'It is in a vulnerable position as far as the wind is concerned...We had to ferry water up to the site, which meant the engines doing a relay back to the nearest water hydrant...and coming back with 400 gallons'.

It was rebuilt shortly afterwards in the style of a Captain's Table with plenty of pine, saw meets of the East Sussex and Romney Marsh Hunt, and was popular for Rotary functions and Sunday lunches. On a clear day there are fine views from the dining tables, especially to the west with the gentle humps of the Downs leading to Belle Tout and beyond. From the car parks the Eastbourne Astronomical Society observed further - the Kohoutek Comet in 1975 and Hale-Bopp in 1997.

Proposals to build a luxury hotel complex here, which many locals thought would spoil Beachy Head, fell through with the recession, and the site was taken over in June 1993 by brewery giant Whitbread.

The hotel reopened in the spring of 1994, following a £650 000 refit, with an enlarged Beachy Head Countryside Centre which had planned extra activities for Christmas 1994, with displays of Sussex paintings, wood-turned items by Barrie Smith, storyteller Pat Brown in attendance to entertain the children, and author David Arscott to sign copies of his books.[11] On 10 December 1994, however, the hotel burnt to the ground again, the fire starting over the lunch hour in the rubbish area near the kitchens. Strong winds rushed the flames through the building and, although over 100 customers and staff escaped safely, the fire essentially burnt itself out.[12]

Without delay Whitbread's built an enlarged Brewer's Fayre restaurant and bar to reopen the following summer. Included was the Eastbourne Borough Council's Beachy Head Countryside Centre, opened by Mayor Ron Parsons and Lord Nathan in April 1996. It has 3-D colour slides, a "talking shepherd", a touch screen computer, a micrarium, and a mock cliff face to help explain the cliffs and the Downs. There is a regular summer bus service from Eastbourne front.

About the same time the police and coastguard hut, with its prominent radio aerial, was rebuilt alongside the hotel car park. It had been on the opposite side of the road - by the site of the original signal station - for many years. Later the "Samaritans" telephone box was also moved to the hotel side of the road.

The Beachy Head Hotel hosts the East Sussex Hounds in 1924

At Monkey Island, between 350m and 550m east from the lighthouse, the cliffs vary in height from 150m to 160m, and provide an obvious spot for beacons and bonfires. It is said the Romans built a Great Beacon Tower here, and warning of the Spanish Armada (first sighted off Sussex from Selsey at 1100h on 25 July 1588) was given from Beachy Head (see Bonfires and Beacons in Chapter 2).

The cliffs abut the sea in a jumbled magnificence of rock: here a white, vertical overhang, there sweeping down in a tumbled heap of loose chalk. The golden beauty, the scent of the flowers and the busying of insects in summer are well expressed in Arthur Beckett's *The Spirit of the Downs*. The views are tremendous, with many a sail and ship to be observed. The sea here has so many colours, with the light green platform seen under the sea representing the former extent of the chalk. This is exposed at low tide.

It is said that the height of Beachy Head is perceived not so much from contemplating the cliffs, as by listening to the indistinct murmur of the waves from the cliff top.

To the west it is possible to have glimpses of the lighthouse, appearing magical against the setting sun. Looking back eastwards, the Eastbourne front (with its pier and occasional, and incongruous, tower block) stands out, the Martello towers towards Pevensey Bay can be made out, and the curving inlet of Norman's Bay is obvious from this height, with Hastings in the background.

Nowadays it would be impossible for William Camden to miss Eastbourne. Travelling eastwards in 1580 he came, "...to Cuckmer, a very considerable harbour. Crossing over the promontory called Beach from its gravely beach, we come to Pevensey". So much for Eastbourne in those days.[13]

The now demolished police and coastguards' hut on the cliff side of the road, nearby is the "Samaritans" telephone box, both are now across the road

About 300m east of the lighthouse, the Beachy Head cliffs reach their maximum height of 165m (535 feet), while just inland the ridge of Downs rises to 180m above sea level. Beachy Head may be the highest chalk headland on the south coast, but the highest point of the South Downs is Butser Hill (273m). The county summit of Sussex is the greensand of Black Down near Haslemere.

Beachy Head is one of the finest marine eminences in Europe. According to JD Parry, "It inspires some degree of fear (pronounced by Burke to be essential to the sublime) and pity at the recollected calamities. The view from the summit has an air of sublime grandeur".

At 165m (535feet) Beachy Head is one-and-a-half times the height of St Paul's Cathedral in London (111m, 365 ft), some 100 feet higher than the Cliffs of Dover, and higher than the great spires of Strasbourg and Antwerp Cathedrals. About the same as the Post Office Tower in London, it is dwarfed by Canary Wharf's 240m tower, the 295m of the Thistle North Sea oil platform (of which over half is submerged) and by the Empire State Building, New York, at 1160ft.

Beachy Head, Devil's Chimney and lighthouse in 1986 {J Dann}

Unlike Beachy Head they did not provide the inspiration, in September 1886, for Algernon Swinburne (1837-1909) to pen his ode *To a Seamew*.[14]

> *The lark has no such rapture*
> *Such joy no nightingale.*

Richard Jefferies in his essay, *The Breeze on Beachy Head,* also tells of, "...the glory of these glorious Downs is the breeze. It is air without admixture. The great headland and the whole rib of promontory is windswept and washed with air; the billows of the atmosphere roll over it...".

EV Lucas in *Highways & Byways in Sussex* says, "Eastbourne's glory is Beachy Head, last of the Downs in Sussex. About Beachy Head the South Downs has the best turf, best prospect, best loneliness and the best air".

Beachy Head is beautiful, historic and full of interest, but also acts as a protection for Eastbourne from the prevailing south westerly winds, affording shelter in gales. It is described by the Eastbourne Natural History Society as, "not only in metaphor but also in sober reality the buttress and bulwark of the land". Borough meteorologists, such as Mr WL Peck and Mr Sidney Hall, have repeatedly emphasised that "a great deal of the good weather in Eastbourne can be attributed to the Downs. They act as a natural barrier and we are extremely lucky." In practical terms Eastbourne usually tops the sunshine league chart for mainland resorts - in 1976 it had a total of 2101.7 hours of sun, and 2158 in 1911.

A regular spot for a coastguard exercise near Beachy Head's summit

Edward Lear (1812-1888) of comic verse fame, but also a talented painter, produced an oil on canvas picture of "Beachy Head". What was missing in his day is the added colour imparted to the scene by hang gliders. On suitable days there can be over 20 jumping off or coming in to land.

King Edward VII visited Beachy Head in 1904 and met Chief Officer George Hogben of the coastguards' station.

Recently attempts have been made to enable more visitors experience the beauty and variety of the views in safety. A path for the disabled was given the go-ahead in 1986 and opened in 1988 (see Walks around Beachy Head, Chapter 10).

Coming to within 250m east of the lighthouse we are just past the highest point of the cliffs, although there is little change over the next few hundred metres. Standing near the edge and looking downwards and to the west it is possible to see the lighthouse rising from the sea away from the cliffs, and further along the coastline the indentations and undulations of the cliffs as they gradually fall in height, only to rise again at Belle Tout, the site of the old lighthouse. The closely cropped grassland and even contours provide a most peaceful scene.

Wholesale development of this coast was only prevented by the many lovers of the Downs, such as the Society of Sussex Downsmen led by the author Arthur Beckett, "who loved the view". Their determination to keep Beachy Head unspoilt was spurred on by the example of Peacehaven - a well intentioned scheme, but nonetheless a despoliation they were determined to prevent elsewhere.

The first brave step, however, was taken by Eastbourne Corporation in 1926, when it completed the Downs purchase. An area of 4100.076 acres (1700 hectares), which included Beachy Head and its hinterland, was bought at a cost of £91 291/1s/7d, in other words about £22 per acre. This is still in the custodianship of the Eastbourne Borough Council, or its successors, and so far has remained an open space and, in the main, is open to all.

On 29 October 1929 the Duke and Duchess of York (later King George VI and Queen Elizabeth) unveiled plaques set in a stone seat to commemorate the purchase. These were damaged during the 1939-45 War and removed. Happily they have been restored and the Duke of Devonshire was present on 21 November 1979 for an occasion to celebrate their replacement. They are across the road from the coastguard building, slightly east of the hotel. The old Lloyd's signalling station is further to the west (see Chapter 4 on Coastguards and Signals).

The Sussex Heritage Coast and the line of cliffs between Eastbourne and Seaford were among the 34 stretches of coastline selected by the Countryside Commission in 1967 as of outstanding beauty. On 15 July 1972 Lord Shawcross officially opened the South Downs Way. This was the Countryside Commission's first long distance combined walking and bridle path, an 80-mile walkers' and riders' route from Beachy Head to the Hampshire border, and since extended. Vigilance is still required, especially when faced with the dilemma of "maximising resources" without minimising the quality of life. In 1984 Cllr (now Sir) John Chatfield, the leader of the East Sussex County Council, was grateful for representations from the public to ensure safeguarding of the County's heritage against any form of oil or gas exploration.

A 1989 report compiled for Eastbourne Borough Council suggested that more should be done to attract the visitor and to tap every possible source of income. Car parks should be built and a charge made; land should be changed to permanent pasture, with safe, well maintained and signposted paths; an assistant to Alan Ferguson (the Ranger in 1989) be employed, and a Visitor Centre set up.

The Sussex Downs Conservation Board, set up in 1992 for five years, had an annual budget in excess of £1m to protect this Area of Outstanding Natural Beauty, and encourage enjoyment of the Downs. It consisted of representatives of the Countryside Commission, and local County, District and Borough councillors.

To continue along the cliffs, at 200-250m east of the lighthouse the cliff face is vertical for about 60m followed by a more gradual slope - a rampart at the cliff base formed by repeated falls of chalk.

Another 50m west is the feature known as Gun Gardens, where there was a Police telephone box. The name of this site probably relates to military ordnance in the time of Napoleon, but as will unfold, Beachy Head was used as a vantage point for many other battles. (See Chapter 8)

At 200m east of the lighthouse the cliffs are almost sheer, being broken only by two steeply sloping ledges near the base.

Within 150m of the lighthouse the cliffs are fissured and irregular with innumerable small ledges and inclines on the cliff face. Columns of chalk stand out and many of the pillars are given names, such as Devil's Chimney, which will be mentioned in the chapter on climbing,

There is usually low fencing along part of these cliffs, to save the public tripping over the irregular ground, or falling over crumbling cliff edge.

Police Downs Ranger on Jumbo in the 1960s {E Worsfold}

The force of the waves and shingle, coupled with pressure changes in the rock crevices and the effects of rain and frost, undermine and erode the cliffs, and this weathering alters the outline from year to year. Each year on average 0.5m (18 inches) of cliff edge is lost, although the rate fluctuates. The resultant rock falls mean that even the sheerest cliff will often have a buttress of fallen boulders at the base, sometimes running almost 30m (100 feet) up the cliff face.

Brabant writes, "To appreciate the full grandeur of Beachy Head the visitor should [also] walk along the beach"[15] (see Chapter 10). If you are walking at the base of the cliffs, where in parts the overhang of the cliffs is obvious, it is sensible not to get too close. In August 1983 a few rotting items of male clothing were found partly buried under an enormous rock fall at the foot of the cliffs about here. The clothing and a set of keys were identified as belonging to a 65-year-old Brighton man who had been missing since the previous January. At an inquest in 1986 it was assumed that he could be under 1500 tons of rock, but it was not thought feasible to attempt any further exploration.[16]

At this point the Downland on the cliff top is also fissured and the cracks can open up alarmingly in times of drought. In July 1976 a 12-year-old girl fell 100 feet down a fissure as described in Chapter 7.

Lloyd's Signalman's Cottage, from the Beachy Head Hotel looking west in 1987

From 1897 a bungalow, built by Lloyd's, lay between the hotel and the bus stop, on the sea side of the road. It was referred to as the "Signalman's" or "Watchman's Cottage", and from 1972-86 was run as a Natural History Centre by the Eastbourne Natural History & Archaeological Society displaying the history, flora, and fauna of the Downs. The Sussex Wildlife Trust and the local Council later ran it as a Countryside Centre until it was destroyed by arson in 1992. This function has been taken over by the new Centre, alongside the hotel.

The Lighthouse (see Lights and Lighthouses, Chapter 2)

The lighthouse continues as one of the attractions of the area. It was used as a mark for the 1951 Daily Express Air Race, Sir Francis Chichester sailed by in Gypsy Moth IV on 4 July 1967, and it has long been a favourite holiday view with visitors, and once seen is seldom forgotten.

It adds a sense of scale to the scene, looking like a toy from the cliff top despite being almost 40m (140 feet) high. It is not advised to view the lighthouse from directly above, the cliff here is often crumbly, but you know it is there by the telelink and electricity supply covers set into the Downs. What you might not know is that Friedrich Engels (1820-95) had his ashes scattered off Beachy Head.

West of the lighthouse the cliffs fall in height from about 145m to less than 120m over a quarter of a mile. These may not be the highest cliffs, but the face is sheer except where falls of chalk have heaped boulders to a height of 15m at the base. The Downs dip and rise before dropping down before Belle Tout.

The 1979 film *Quadrophenia,* inspired by 1960s' battles between Mods and Rockers, with the music of The Who, has a scene in which a moped is ridden off the top of Beachy Head. In the 1987 James Bond film *The Living Daylights,* with Timothy Dalton as 007, a flaming Land Rover was driven off these cliffs. The burnt-out vehicle even became a tourist attraction on the beach. Beachy Head also featured in the 1980 film *Hopscotch* starring Walter Matthau and Glenda Jackson, *The Return of Sherlock Holmes* in 1986, a Dick Barton film, and innumerable TV commercials from Foster's Lager, Toshiba photocopiers, to Fiat cars.

Troops going down the cliff face as part of a Royal Engineer's exercise to recover dumped cars {Brighton Evening Argus}

Leaving the lighthouse behind to walk along the gently undulating grassy way, with scrub alongside the road, the cliffs are not only vertical, but the cliff edge is irregular with deep incisions into the Downs, revealing projecting buffs. In 1974, a 20-year-old motor cyclist riding parallel to the cliff edge near here failed to notice an indentation in time to save him driving into the gap.

The road swings inland so that at one point it is 500m from the cliff, further than at any point since Cow Gap, although the distance averages 300m. There are not so many car lay-bys just here and a high gorse-covered slope, on the coastal side of the road, does not make for easy direct access to the cliffs.

At some 300m west of the lighthouse there is a dip in the Downs called Shooter's Bottom. The name derives from naval gunnery practice, firing at a hidden target as part of gun laying spotters' training. Many shells went into the face of the cliff, are still being uncovered by cliff falls, and need to be detonated by bomb squad officers.

It is almost impossible to imagine such happenings amid the calm and quiet of to-day's Downs. The main dangers now are from changes in husbandry, or the tourist wearing away the springy Downland turf, which contains a great variety of plants, including at least eight species of orchid (see Chapter 9). In recent years the Eastbourne Council, encouraged by Councillor Maurice Skilton, have appointed a Downs Ranger (David Pearce in 1997) who traverses the area in a Land Rover and whose main job is conservation and protecting the environment.

For many years the police provided a mounted Downs Ranger who rode the Downs, maintaining the peace. PC Henry Poole patrolled from 1929 to 1953, his most famous horse being "Princess Patricia," and he was succeeded by PC Harry Ward. The last mounted Downs Ranger was PC Jack Williams who took over the 17½-hands dapple-grey "Jumbo" in 1963. The horses were stabled in the police and coastguard building. Later Beachy Head was patrolled by an area beat constable whose responsibility stretched from Birling Gap to Meads in Eastbourne. PC Ian Tubb, the Downs Ranger in 1979, explained that his main work was dealing with summer visitors, who would park and light fires on the Downland, but he did get involved in falls from the cliffs (see Appendix 2).

It is equally difficult to believe that horse racing once took place on the Beachy Head Downs, just near the present Bullock Down. Eastbourne held race meetings in 1729, 1737 and again from 1866 to 1875. Chambers didn't think much of the race followers, "...neither Eastbourne nor Sussex contributed to the contingent of 'ladies' and 'gentlemen' who disfigured our Downs". There was also a polo ground on Long Down north of the bridle path between Black Robin and Bullock Down Farms. It was last mentioned in 1935.[17]

In the past the Downs were a favourite place to exercise horses, and horse riding on the Downs was a favourite pastime; the smooth, elastic turf makes both walking and riding a delight.

Looking inland an obvious "Dew Pond" can be seen across the road, near to *Hodcombe,* a private residence. In the distance is the village of Friston on the far hill, with its grey water tower standing 75 feet high.

Coming up to 800m west of the lighthouse, almost half way to Belle Tout, the cliff face remains vertical and although the height is only around 80-100m the cliffs do ensure a direct fall to the beach. It is wise to keep away from the cliff edge which can overhang, yet every year people will sit near the edge.

About 150m east of Belle Tout, where the cliffs are perhaps 50m in height, the road runs within ten metres of the cliff edge and, until earth banks were built up at the back of the car park over the last few years, it was a fairly level drive off the road across grassland to reach the edge (see Chapter 5). The first record of a car going over is on 10 June 1908, and since then cars and the Downs have had an uneasy relationship. On 21 April 1938 a motorist was fined 25p for driving furiously on the Downs, and on both 5 and 8 of August 1938 motorists were prosecuted at Eastbourne magistrates' court for driving offences on the Downs.[18]

A few of the cars brought up in November 1992. They included a Rolls Royce, stolen from a Crawley hotel on 8 August 1992, looking a Silver Shadow of what it had been, particularly after being dropped 100 feet out of the sling at the first attempt. This is just by the car park near Belle Tout, which is in the background

During PC Ward's time as Downs Ranger a Triumph TR3 was stolen in London and pushed over Beachy Head. The student owner asked PC Ward if it would be possible to get it up because he only had Third Party Insurance. The Ranger, pointing down to the wreck said, 'There it is. What do you think?'

In the 1970s a VW Beetle was driven over, but remained upright in remarkably good condition. Some time later VW were running a nationwide publicity campaign, "Underneath it's still a Volkswagen" and, in view of the slight damage to this car, locally it was suggested that the slogan should be rephrased to "At the bottom it's still a VW".[19]

Belle Tout (see Lights and Lighthouses, Chapter 2)

This brings the walk to Belle Tout where the Downs rise again to about 85m (275 feet) above sea level. On top of the mound is the old Belle Tout lighthouse, which shone from 1828 to 1902. It is now a private residence.

The name is not French, but is derived from its ancient associations.[20] "Bel" (as it appears on maps into the 1820s) is the name of an early pagan deity, and "Toot" is Saxon for "look-out" (there is a Toot Rock near Hastings) - and the second "t" is pronounced.

On the apex are the remains of a prehistoric earthwork (mostly eroded away) within the lines of which the lighthouse was built. The site has had associations with mankind for thousands of years. There was an Iron Age camp at the summit, which must have been well away from the sea at the time, and just to the west is evidence of Bronze Age habitation. The only Beaker people's site in south east England, of some 2000 BC, was identified at Belle Tout in 1968.

The old Belle Tout lighthouse in the 1920s, with the Seven Sisters to the left

It was in 1968 that Bradley confirmed the presence of a 250-foot deep shaft running down to the greensand. It had footholds and matched those of North German origin. In February 1971 a fall of cliff, between Belle Tout and Birling Gap, exposed another prehistoric well shaft, again with footmarks, suggesting long term habitation of the site. Post holes and axe heads have also been found in the area.[21, 22, 23, 24, 25]

A line of barrows, or burial mounds, (marked *Tumuli* on maps) runs from Beachy Head to Willingdon Hill, nearly five miles inland. The common type here is the bowl barrow, where a ditch is dug around the burial and the earth piled over, giving a bowl-shaped heap. In 1806 four gold bracelets were found on the Wish Tower beach along with palstaves, celts and part of a Bronze Age sword.

In more recent times Belle Tout was the site of a not too successful lighthouse. When, in 1902, it was superseded by the present lighthouse at the foot of the cliffs the Belle Tout lighthouse was sold as, "a small, substantial 3-storey building".

It must have been a typical pastoral scene in the first few decades of the 20th century, and the Sussex County Magazine has a picture of a team of docile Sussex oxen ploughing on the slope inland of the Belle Tout lighthouse.[26]

In 1923 the distinguished neurologist, Sir James Purves-Stewart, bought the site for £1500. Sir James was assured by geologists that the ex-lighthouse would not be eroded for 600 years; apparently it had been 34m (115 ft) from the edge in 1835 and was 30m in 1890. Satisfied, Sir James built an approach road, installed an electric generator, converted the lantern room into a sun lounge, entertained Lord Chief Justice Stewart and, in 1935, King George V and Queen Mary.

War-ravaged Belle Tout ex-lighthouse in 1945, looking west at the Seven Sisters

The old lighthouse looks unlikely to last another 100 years. A Trinity House drawing by J Walker in 1835 shows that the living quarters of the Belle Tout lighthouse were 107 feet 8 inches from the cliff edge. In 1986 the same point was 52 feet 4 inches from the edge (measured by Tom McAll), and the nearest point of the lighthouse tower to the cliff edge was 38 feet. On this basis, assuming steady erosion, the cliff edge will reach the tower about 2100; however, erosion occurs in an irregular fashion. In 1893 alone a 9m (30 ft) width of cliff, stretching over 130m (400 ft) in length fell to the west of the lighthouse.

During the 1939-45 War it received extensive damage. Although bombs dropped nearby on 23 November 1940, the destruction was almost entirely as a result of gunnery practice. A target on rails was erected in the valley between the main headland and Belle Tout, and guns of every description fired live ammunition at it, and any shells which missed went harmlessly out to sea, except for the occasional one that hit the lighthouse. When the Canadians arrived they showed little respect for a disused lighthouse and by 1944 it was a wreck.

In 1948 Sir James, having received £5000 war compensation, offered it to the Eastbourne Borough Council, but it remained in a ruinous condition until Dr Edward Revill Cullinan leased the ex-lighthouse and started rebuilding in August 1956. It is said that Dr Cullinan, unable to afford a copper dome, advertised for a secondhand redundant one. The only reply came from Argentina with a remarkable offer of a dome of exactly the dimensions required - and free.

Belle Tout still very ex-lighthouse, but made sound in 1960, looking westward

Unfortunately, after careful examination of the transaction, Dr Cullinan found that it would cost more to transport the dome from Argentina than his budget for all the repairs, so he had to decline the offer.

Dr Cullinan first put it up for sale in September 1962 at £15 000 and since Dorothea, his widow, sold the lease the old lighthouse has changed hands on a number of occasions. Notwithstanding a macabre incident on 18 October 1967, when a tenant hung himself from the staircase, it has been improved into a desirable private dwelling and was again up for sale in 1985 - this time at £50 000.

25

In 1986 the lighthouse and surrounds were upgraded by the BBC at a cost, so it was rumoured, of £250 000, to use for three weeks' film location work, in the TV series "Life and Loves of a She-Devil," (from the novel by Fay Weldon) starring Patricia Hodge and Dennis Waterman.

Landscape gardener David Wells was awarded the contract to reconstruct the garden and it was pretty enough until the trees were blown down and it reverted much to its old state.[27] Back in private hands, in June 1988 the lantern room was restored as a replica of the original, but for use as a handsome summer lounge.

On most sunny days in the summer sunbathers, painters and walkers gather around the Belle Tout summit. Looking to the east there is a charming view of the new lighthouse peeping round the wall of the cliffs, the light flashing twice every 20 seconds, and westward the gorse covered Downs slope to the road and Birling Gap with the world famous lines of the Seven Sisters beyond.

A new lantern room/sun lounge about to be placed on top of the old Belle Tout lighthouse, June 1988 {Beckett Newspapers}

The humps of the cliffs, such as Belle Tout, represent the more erosion-resistant parts of the Downs and so perhaps after all it could be another century before the edifice topples from its perch. Let's hope so, for in December 1994 the old lighthouse, now a Grade II listed building, with its "4 double bedrooms, open plan living area with olive wood floor, 2 garages and walled garden", was up for sale at £350 000.

There are sketchy plans to move Belle Tout, but below it at present there is a clump of trees, Horseshoe Plantation, and across the road, to the left, is Cornish

Farm. The concrete road running over the fields was built during the 1939-45 war. Some of the pathways through the fields were Roman tracks, and further to the right is a low flint wall built by French prisoners-of-war in Napoleonic times.

Birling Gap (see also Coastguards, Chapter 4)

From Belle Tout you walk down to Birling Gap along gorse-lined tracks, often blackened with scars of summer fires, which on 23 May 1956 destroyed 25 acres.

About half way down there was a coastguard lookout now replaced by a National Trust cairn. The white-painted Dieppe/Newhaven ferry often hoves into view, and wonderful views of the gleaming white Seven Sisters cliffs appear with Cuckmere Haven and Seaford Head in the background. As we approach Birling Gap, where there is a car park and another pub welcomes us, the road curves on to East Dean and the main Brighton road.

The *Sussex County Magazine* states that Birling is Gaelic for boat,[28] but most believe the name comes from a Saxon tribe the "Beorls" who were raiders and settled at the site of Birling Manor. In the 13th century the manor of Birling belonged to the great family of Bardolf. Over the years there have been many variations in the spelling of this means of access to the sea - Berlin, Berlingate, Byrlinge Gappe to mention a few.

Birling Gap has had many experiences of war, from the Danes in the Dark Ages, the Spanish in the 16th century, the French from the 14th to the 18th centuries, and more recently the Germans (see Beachy Head at War, Chapter 8). The 19th century saw it used as a gap in the cliffs where a submarine cable could be landed and perhaps help to bind nations together in enlightened amity.

Fishing was a considerable industry before the 1914-18 war. In the summer months fishermen would lay lobster and crab pots off the Beachy Head ledge, at Birling Gap, and on the Horse rocks near the Royal Sovereign.[29] If they had a good catch they celebrated at the bungalow hotel. To-day only a lone fisherman, Brian Johnson, keeps his open boat at Birling Gap, whereas the Birling Gap Hotel, there for a century, has been modernised in recent years and does well.

Until 1939 there was a 9-hole golf course at Birling Gap. The Birling Manor course, opened in 1894, was popular with the locals. Mrs Joyce Donkin, who recalls she often played golf there before 1939, says it was used for ammunition storage during the 1939-45 war, and afterwards returned to farmland.

Rudyard Kipling was among those who subscribed to a purchase fund initiated by the Society of Sussex Downsmen in the 1920s to save the Crowlink Valley from the speculative builder. Birling Gap was bought by the National Trust in 1982, with the help of a legacy by Miss Mabel Arbuthnot. This made a total of 700 acres (283 hectares) of NT land when added to the Seven Sisters coastline, which it had owned since before the 1939-45 War.

It was the National Trust's intention to "tidy up" Birling Gap by knocking down most of the buildings and replacing them with a refreshment block and toilets. It has to be said that some of the buildings had become run down and were an eyesore, but when a cottage *White Horses* was demolished to make way for a toilet block in 1985 there was an outcry. Finally, the Collins' family bought up the hotel and two years later the National Trust shelved their demolition plans.

Birling Gap, 1911. The hotel just appears on the left and the coastguard cottages are left centre. The end cottages, rocket house, boat and watch house have gone

The Gap is popular for bathing. The shoreline is shingle, with a smidgen of sand, interspersed with falls of whiter than white chalk. Access to the beach is by means of temporary wooden steps and planks supported by scaffolding. The steps are sometimes closed in the winter or damaged by storms, and have to be replaced every few years as the cliff is worn away. Since 1986 an inshore boat has been provided by the local initiative of the Birling Gap Safety Boat Association to assist any small craft or bathers in difficulties, and in 1995 the beach won a Seaside Award from the Tidy Britain Group.

Towards the east are rock pools with crystal clear water, where prawns and shrimps and hermit crabs may be found. In deeper waters mullet and sea bass are abundant in season, especially around submerged wrecks (see Natural History, Chapter 9).

A famous shipwreck just off here was the Spanish Prize-of-War, *Nympha Americana,* which went ashore "between Berlin Gap and the Cuckmer" in 1747, while on tow (see Shipwrecks, Chapter 3). Its rich cargo was an attraction to the locals and one looter was shot dead, "yet people will continue to venture". It also provided an example of a cliff fall when a watcher fell from the top of the cliff.

Cars manage to go over the cliffs here, too. On 30 March 1946 a car with two RAF officers and two women plunged over a cliff at Birling Gap. One officer leapt from the driver's seat just before it went over the edge, and the others got away with bruises and one broken collar bone.

There were more lucky escapes when a lorry careered over the cliffs at Birling Gap on 24 August 1989. A tow-rope had snapped and the vehicle somersaulted onto the beach, just missing startled holidaymakers.

Birling Gap had an outbreak of crop circles[30] in June 1994, but otherwise is the meeting of roads from Eastbourne and East Dean. It has a concoction of buildings - old coastguard cottages, coastguard huts, modern houses, the Birling Gap Hotel - all now in some danger of being left to fall into the sea.

The cliffs show ample evidence of erosion at the Gap. You can see a stone wall coming to a jagged stop at the cliff edge and there is encroachment of the cliff edge into the gardens of the hotel and other houses, exposing old drainpipes.

Birling Gap looking east from the Seven Sisters, 1986. The Birling Gap Hotel is centre left. The steps to the beach are to the right and the coastguard lookout is above on the skyline. The coastguard cottages in the centre have since lost another section nearest the sea {Beckett Newspapers}

Erosion and weathering affect all sea cliffs and change the coastal outline, as headlands are battered and undercut by the waves and split by frost. The lower chalk tends to be the hardest and the headlands are most resistant to weathering.

Many of the dips in the cliffs are made of a softer chalk and gravel and it is because they are the weakest parts that they form the indentations and valleys.

In the last Ice Age of over 10 000 years ago the pack ice did not reach to the present south coast, but the area was cold, with snow on the hills most of the year. In winter any water in the chalk froze, and the expansion broke up the rock. During summer the surface layers thawed and slid downhill. These broken-up rocks, known as Coombe Deposits, were carried for deposition in the river valleys. In the parts where the chalk has been dissolved away there are many flints.

Coombe Deposits are softer than chalk and are eroded away quicker. The cross section of the hills and valleys provided by the Seven Sisters cliffs near Birling Gap shows the slightly browner, rubbly deposits filling up the valleys. When the Channel broke through some 10 000 years ago, sea erosion began.

Birling Gap steps near collapse in January gales,1994 {Beckett Newspapers}

In 1920 the Royal Commission on Coast Erosion estimated an annual rate of loss of 0.5m (18 inches) at Beachy Head. Erosion is variable, on average, 50 000 tonnes of chalk fall every year, by the gram and occasionally by the tonne. There were great falls in 1813, 1848, 1853, 1893 and 1913, and 89 000 tons fell at Belle Tout on 8 October 1896. In the 1813 fall the Vicar of East Dean, Mr Gardener, was walking along the cliff edge when he noticed a crack appearing to his landward side. With great presence of mind he jumped over the gap, just before the mass of cliff on which he had been standing, crashed to the beach below.

Nowadays it is to be hoped that such falls are avoided by monitoring the state of the cliffs and taking measures designed to avoid such dramatic and dangerous falls. In the past drastic actions have been taken, the blasting operation near Holywell has already been mentioned and in 1977 an unsafe sliver of cliff just east of Birling Gap was blown away with the help of the Army.

Most of the loss of coastline is insidious, but it is well demonstrated at Birling Gap. In the 19th century it was possible to climb up a steep slope from the beach to the Downs. As late as 1937 there was as much land from the end coastguard cottage to the cliff edge, as the length of the terrace. In March 1972 the officer's cottage, called *Leander,* at the sea end of the coastguard terrace, was within five feet of the edge at a time when there had been 21 feet of erosion at that point between 1970 and 1971. This end cottage was demolished in August 1972, and in December 1994 the next house of the terrace row, now called *Crangon Cottages,* had to be demolished and the end wall shored up.

Other buildings at Birling Gap have long since gone. There was a long narrow building along the south wall of the cottage's gardens used for coastguard rocket equipment, and a boathouse, which became unsafe and were demolished in 1928. A watch room in front of the Birling Gap Hotel, which also housed coastguard materials, was destroyed during the 1939-45 war.

Until November 1967 you could walk from Belle Tout to the Seven Sisters along the cliff edge in front of the Birling Gap Hotel.

To express the rate of erosion another way: in 1898 the sea end of the row of cottages was 84m (276 ft) from the cliff edge, in 1926 it was 191 feet, and in 1986 only 66 feet (Tom McAll). In 1898 the stone-built garden wall around the coastguard cottages was

Blowing up unstable, dangerous cliffs near Birling Gap in 1977. On the left is the eroded edge of the coastguard cottages' wall {Beckett Newspapers}

square and whole; the NW and SE sides measured 300 feet, and the SW and NE sides 250 feet. By 1926 the southern corner had been eroded, and by 1986 only 142 feet remained of the SE side.

In 1994 Wealden District Council introduced for discussion a policy of "Managed Retreat", in conjunction with Shoreline Management Plans. Some inhabitants of the Gap believe this is a handle for doing as little as possible, and that without a boulder revetment the houses and pub will drop into the sea in about 20 years' time.

Graham Collins fears that the part of the Birling Gap Hotel nearest the cliff has only about 15 years, although the more recently built sections are to the landward side and could possibly continue longer.

A 180m-long rock wall at the foot of the cliffs and costing £340 000, was one of the Council's options, but the National Trust and the Sussex Downs Conservation Board said they wished no form of engineering work. The Gap suffered severe cliff falls in the 1995-96 winter, putting the steps out of action. Temporary steps were not an option because there was no firm base, and as a result some six months went by without access.

So it is a constantly changing scene, which helps to make the whole walk from Eastbourne to Birling Gap a marvellous part of the South Downs Way. The way on from the Gap, over the Seven Sisters, past Crowlink, and down to Cuckmere Haven is not strictly part of "Beachy Head", none the less it is next door and will be briefly mentioned in Chapter 10 on Walks around Beachy Head.

From Meads to Birling Gap is about 5 miles and the traverse of the Seven Sisters to Exceat is a further 5-6 miles. The undulations, some steep, mean that it may take longer than you thought, but time passes quickly with the vast expanse of sea on your left, the Downs stretching away inland and a wonderful walk ahead. There is also the fascination of the changing seasons: the stimulation of winter's white horses on grey surging waves, to the shimmering reflections and intense colours - every shade of green and blue - all on a still summer's day.

2 LIGHTS AND LIGHTHOUSES, BEACONS AND BONFIRES

A great attraction at Beachy Head is the red and white-banded lighthouse, looking toy-like from the top of the cliffs, despite being some 40m high. The view is well-known at home and abroad and graces many a calendar and notelet. Locally the logo of a lighthouse is used in many enterprises, from Clear View Rental & Relay of Seaford to the Beachy Head Hotel itself, and even finds a rôle as a symbol to record the response to Eastbourne's Publicity Appeal Fund. There is a model of the lighthouse in the Countryside Centre at Beachy Head.

Looking up at the lighthouse from the beach
{Eastbourne Tourism & Leisure}

Beachy Head was notorious for its dangerous currents, and the Venetians called it Caput Doble, the Devil's Headland. A shelf of hard rock with jagged projections rising above low water is still a well-recognised maritime danger between Birling Gap and Eastbourne and likely to tear out the hull of any vessel driven or drifting on to it (see Shipwrecks, Chapter 3).

It is said there was "a light" at Beachy Head as early as 1670, shortly before the building of Winstanley's 1698 Eddystone lighthouse. In the reign of William and Mary a 1691 petition of Thomas Offley stated, "It sheweth that a great number of ships have been heretofore lost and some are lost every year near 'the Beachy' in Sussex being a very dangerous coast in the dark; and whereas nothing is so good to prevent the same loss as a lighthouse." This plea was referred by Her Majesty to the Trinity House, Deptford Strand, where it stagnated for more than 100 years, but the single-handed efforts of Parson Darby of East Dean to prevent shipwrecks must not be forgotten.

Parson Darby's Cave

Until recent years it was possible to discern in the cliffs, near Belle Tout, a vertical shaft - all that remained of what was known in the district as "Parson Darby's Cave" or "Darby's Hole". It was a long-lasting piece of evidence for a tale of folk lore that has an appeal to the heart and the imagination.

Jonathan Darby of Sussex stock, but born at Appleby in Westmorland in 1667, married Ann Segar at the age of 14 and in 1683 they moved to Oxford. He obtained his BA in 1689 and his Master's degree in 1704. He and his wife had five children, three dying young. He accepted the living at East Dean on 11 February 1705 and took up the appointment the next year.

Soon he was writing to the Admiralty complaining that French vessels had appeared off Birling Gap, and had put men ashore. "They fell upon my Lord Pelham's flock at Chinting ... but the Customs Officers ... drove them back. They came to Crowlink ... and there they plundered the house."[1]

The story goes that after the shipwreck of an 800-ton schooner, with the loss of all her crew, he was fired with the urge to give practical help to such mariners. Working with chisel, pick and axe, he created a series of tunnels with a chalk staircase from the beach. One of the caves had a balcony some 6m (20 ft) above the highest water, reached through a chimney from the Downs, and Darby fastened a light above the balcony to warn unsuspecting vessels of the rocky outcrop below the surface and helped to save the lives of many a sailor. It is recounted that 12 Dutchmen were saved on one occasion.

In the 19th century there was a rumour that Parson Darby had been driven to his isolated watches to escape from a violent-tongued Xantippe of a wife, and Parry writes that Darby "had a termagant wife", but it appears to be a tale unfounded on fact and repeated for its jocular effect. In fact, he was "desolate" after his wife's death in December 1723 and died at the age of 59. In East Dean churchyard his grave is marked by a lichened slab inscribed,

"Here lies the body of
Parson Darby M.A. Oxon
who died on 26th October 1726
He was the sailors' friend."

Francis Grose, an Army officer in the area about 1795, sketched the cave. It is clear from his drawings that it was extensive with reasonably sized "rooms".

In 1899 Darby's Hole was described as 20 minutes' walk east from Birling Gap, "a genuine chimney is provided with a rope ... (can) pass through the trapdoor into the first floor dining room. A series of smuggler's steps ... take one to the next floor. Callers are asked to sign their names in the visitors' book." The four-foot high opening in the cliff was clearly visible in the early years of the 20th century.

AR Hope Moncrieff says that Darby's Hole consisted of "a staircase and cavern in two compartments hollowed out of the solid rock".

Miss Jay gave a talk to the Eastbourne Natural History Society in March 1914 in which she describes walking about a mile eastwards from Birling Gap, climbing a ladder from the beach to a narrow ledge from which a chimney-shaped hole led to the cave proper. She had to clamber up the chimney, using notches for her feet, while holding on to a rope, which was suspended from a ring and staple driven into the chalk above.

Entry to Darby's Hole,1899, the steps can be seen {Central Library Eastbourne}

'The chimney would just admit one person. At the top there were four or five roughly cut steps which led to the "Hall" and from where you could look out of an arched window, which Darby had enlarged from its smuggling days, and which lit up the Hall fairly well. The window was about 50 foot above the beach. The Hall would have held up to 35 persons. There were two alcoves in the Hall, one was probably made by the smugglers for defence purposes and could have held a large boulder to block it up. The other alcove was used by Darby for his lantern store.

At the far end of the hall, the wall (about 15 foot high) had footholds for the smugglers, but Darby had cut a passage in an upward semicircular fashion to the room above. This second "room" must have provided the smugglers with a safe retreat and store and was known as Darby's bedroom. A wide, low-roofed tunnel led from the bedroom and connected to a smaller cave further inland which had a blackened roof from the candle smoke.' Miss Jay doubted whether this led to any further caves and eventually to the surface of the Downs, 'If it had the access had filled in over the years'.

It seems clear that smugglers first carved out the cave, by enlarging existing fissures in the chalk. Parson Darby altered the internal arrangements making a larger window and easing the access - which smugglers were unlikely to do.

After cliff falls in 1916, entrance to the cave became almost impossible. One of Darby's successors, the Revd AA Evans, writing in the 1930s, says that, "... the entrance of the cave is quite washed away, but by means of a ladder the visitor can get within and see the chisel and axe marks clearly visible on the walls".

Apart from Parson Darby's valiant, but no doubt cold, wet watches, little else was done to prevent shipwrecks. A Mr Willard is said to have designed a rescue apparatus at Birling Gap, but it is doubtful if it saved anyone (see Shipwrecks Chapter 3).

Despite William Congreve's verse, the *Mourning Bride,* there is no proof that Sussex folk undertook shipwrecking on any scale, but like most people living precariously by the sea, they were not averse to taking the opportunity offered by wrecked vessels or free materials washed ashore. It is reputed that ship's timbers were used in the roof beams of the Old Forge at East Dean.[2]

The Owers lightship was fixed off Selsey Bill in 1788 and the Newhaven pier light came next in 1809, but it was the celebrated stranding of the *Thames* that stimulated the provision of a lighthouse. An East Indiaman, she was beached on 3 February 1822 after hitting a rock off Beachy Head. A Manby's mortar was used to fire a line aboard and rescue most of the crew, but the event was the subject of paintings (one by WC Stanfield 1793-1867) and prompted a Captain of the Royal Navy to engage in correspondence on the need to avoid further shipwrecks. He had narrowly escaped disaster at this spot and his vigorously expressed letters were said to be an important stimulus for the Elder Brethren of Trinity House to agree that a permanent lighthouse was needed near Beachy Head.

The Belle Tout Lighthouse (see also Chapter 1)

This brings us to Belle Tout [50° 44' 15" N 0° 12' 58" E] where the Downs rise to form a mound about 85m (270 ft) above sea level. Here a temporary weather-boarded hut was in operation from 1 October 1828 and the permanent lighthouse commenced in 1831 to the design of W Hallett and J Walker.

The *Morning Herald* of 19 November 1832 commented, "... the erection of this Lighthouse was principally brought about through the instrumentality of John

Fuller Esq. of Rose Hill, Sussex, and formerly MP for that county." This was the same "Mad" Jack Fuller (1757-1834), famed as a creator of follies, and fined by the Speaker for using an expletive, who encouraged JMW Turner, one of whose paintings, "The Vale of Ashburnham" shows Beachy Head in the distance.[3]

The lighthouse, 47 feet (15m) high, of some 20 feet diameter, was built of Aberdeen granite, conveyed by ox-teams from Maidstone, on a base 187 feet above high water. First lit on 11 October 1834, the reflectors and Argand fountain lamps were combined on a platform which revolved every two minutes, throwing a light of 22 000 candle power (15 seconds every 2 minutes) which could be seen 23 miles

The Belle Tout lighthouse in 1874. Artistic licence has the sea on the wrong side

out to sea, using two gallons of oil an hour. A guidebook of 1878 advised the visitor to "inspect the massive Belle Tout lighthouse with its thirty oil lamps."

What the guidebook did not mention was that, soon after it came into operation, it became obvious that the lighthouse was defectively sited. In theory the light was visible for miles, in practice it was often obscured because when mists gathered over the sea the beams searched needlessly above. So just when it was wanted, the light was obscured for ships on the sea below, and the shipwrecks continued. As early as 1843, Captain William Cole, Lloyd's Agent at Newhaven, when giving evidence before a Select Committee on Shipwrecks, said that in his opinion Birling Gap remained one of the worst spots on the coast.[4]

There were many examples of wrecks. In the winter of 1854/55, the *William*, a

37

barque with a cargo of wine came ashore at Belle Tout,[5] and in 1869 the brig *Garibaldi* of Colchester struck the rocks just east of Belle Tout. Both crews were saved. The single-funnel, schooner-rigged *Rubens* of 1260 tons bound for Antwerp from Buenos Aries ran aground on the afternoon of 17 January 1876, at Birling Gap in thick fog. After lightening the ship, by throwing overboard part of her cargo of wool, she was towed to Southampton for repairs.

The next month, on Tuesday, 22 February, the barque *Coonatta* of 633 tons from Adelaide, with a cargo of copper and wool, came ashore at Crowlink in dense fog. All the crew and most of the wool and copper ore cargo were saved, but later in the week she broke up after rough weather.[6] The ribs of the *Coonatta* could be seen on the beach for over 100 years. The barque's figurehead was recovered and, as the land hereabouts belonged to the Davies Gilbert family, it was placed in the grounds of Birling Manor, until sold to an American in 1970.

In 1884 the *Hesperian* was even stranded under Belle Tout itself, and the fog-associated incidents continued; on 19 April 1896, the *Westbury* of Bristol, went aground in fog some 550m (600 yds) east of Belle Tout.

Consequently, Trinity House determined to replace the Belle Tout lighthouse. It last shone in October 1902. When the present lighthouse took over "Belle Tout" became a private residence, as described in Chapter 1.

The Beachy Head lighthouse [Fl(2) 20s 25 M, Horn (1) 30s]

The light shall never fail. The unwritten law of Trinity House

That the Belle Tout lighthouse never came up to expectations caused Trinity House to embark on one of their most demanding enterprises at the time - the erection of a lighthouse out from the base of the cliffs on the foreshore below the high water mark. This was after it had been found by experiment that a light nearer the surface of the water shimmered across the sea and aided by reflection off the chalk backcloth could provide a loom of radiance at times when a cliff top light was dulled or lost. So the new lighthouse came to be built just to the west of Devil's Chimney from where it would be visible to shipping over a wider radius.

Mr T Matters was appointed chief engineer, with Mr AH Cross as resident engineer to tackle the enormous constructional problems. In July 1899 an aerial cable was built which carried men and materials from the headland camp down to a platform (similar to a small oil-rig) above the high water mark. Stewart Thorpe writes that many a Sussex lad hung on to the pulleys and was transported from the top of the cliff to the construction platform.[7] The 720 Cornish granite blocks, cut, shaped and checked for fit at the quarry, were conveyed from Eastbourne railway station by a traction engine driven by a local character, Mr H Longley.

Working from the platform a dam was formed around the construction area, which had to be pumped dry after each high tide. Work continued night and day through all weathers until a stone base had been built with steps leading down to the rocks and a mooring for boats allowing a depth of 20 feet during normal tides. Upon this base arose the tower of dovetailed 5-ton granite blocks, which finally reached a height (aerials have since been added) of 38m ($123\frac{1}{2}$ feet) with a base diameter of 47 feet. The light was 103 feet above the spring tide high water mark.

The tower is divided into seven floors reached by a spiral staircase. Originally, below the entrance was a store of 1800 gallons of fresh water, and the next floor was the oil room. Above came the crane room to haul up the provisions which were stored on the next floor, with the living quarters above and the fifth floor was the bedroom. The sixth floor was the service room and the seventh provided the lantern

The lighthouse under construction, 1901, aerial cable and platform to the left

platform. The walls decrease in thickness with increasing height, achieving a larger area of room space at the top. The toilets were at the bottom.

The light came into operation on Thursday, 2 October 1902 and the finishing touches were applied in January 1903. It cost £20 814.

The light source was a mantle mounted on a "Hood" vaporiser which had a candle power of 240 250, later doubled. To fuel the vaporiser with a distillate similar to paraffin oil required 20 minutes work each evening to warm it up ready for ignition. The light threw "two white flashes in quick succession every 20 seconds" which, reflected by the cliff, was visible under almost all conditions for over 16 miles. The optical system comprised six asymmetrical lens panels of

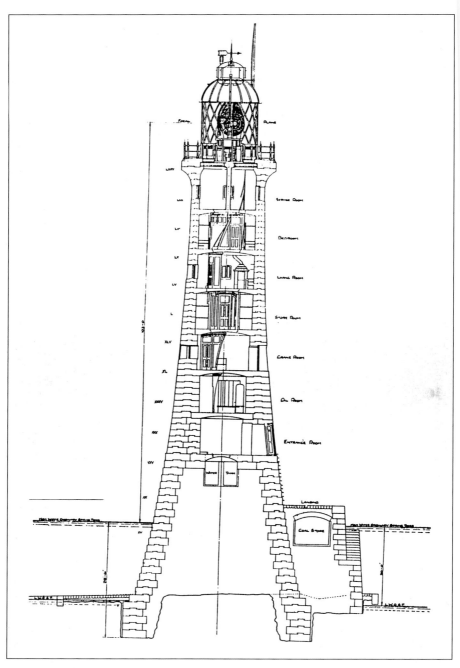

Cross section of the lighthouse {Trinity House engineer's department}

920mm focal length arranged in pairs and mounted on a mercury float pedestal making one complete revolution a minute. The lens clock was weight driven, a run lasting only one hour between rewinds. An explosive fog signal jib mounted on the lantern roof had one report every five minutes. The only electrical power was a battery (charged from a wind driven generator) just sufficient for the fire alarm system - and latterly a TV set.

The "new" lighthouse almost finished, 1902 {Central Library Eastbourne}

The keepers kept four watches every 24 hours and were kept busy winding the clock, lighting the lamp, and pumping up the oil. There was great pride in this technological marvel and James Owen (1847-1928), a local artist of repute, was among many who painted the new Beachy Head lighthouse.

During the 1939-45 war the lighthouse was always manned, but a light was only shown at the request of the Admiralty or Air Ministry. The keepers were exposed to great danger, and the cliffs behind were hit on many occasions yet the lighthouse escaped unscathed.

It is not always known that the red bands were first painted in 1951 as a daymark for inshore shipping - beforehand the bands were black and white. The white sections had been left unpainted in the colour of the natural light granite until in 1980 painters gave the lighthouse a smart red-and-white touch-up.[8]

Electricity had first been used for lighthouses in 1862, and means had been sought for years to supply mains voltage to Beachy Head. Fears of marring the natural beauty and of an aerial cable being severed ensured that the plans were shelved. These fears were not unfounded because the telephone line was cut on several occasions by low flying aircraft, the last on 9 October 1963, and was snapped on three occasions by storms between March 1982 and February 1983.

In 1974 work began on an 11000 volt supply. This included provision of an underground sub-station for transformers and isolating switches, and a take-off chamber cut into the cliff face from where the power line was fed to the lighthouse. Within the tower the power was converted to the usual 240 volt single phase supply. The oil mantle was replaced with a 400 watt mercury iodide lamp, the rotation equipment was also converted, and a 2000 watt nautophone fog horn and a stand-by generator completed the changes. In the advent of total electrical failure there was provision for a "Gaz" lantern to be placed on the spacer top plate of the lantern gallery - after removing the lamp.

The Royal Sovereign Lightship of 1910

On Tuesday, 30 July 1974, the Duke of Edinburgh, Master of Trinity House, sailed to Beachy Head to mark the switch over to electricity after 72 years of oil power. It meant that the keepers no longer had to pump up paraffin from the oil room during their watches. Not only did this ease the work of the lighthouse staff, but as Tony Marsh, a lighthouse keeper in 1974, pointed out, 'The sweeping away of the oil fumes and fug also means considerably more comfort for the three men who spend four weeks at a time on duty there'.

In August 1979 the lighthouse was visited by Eastbourne's respected MP, Mr Ian Gow, with his wife Jane and sons, Charles and Jamie.

A further stage in the history of the lighthouse came on 28 June 1983 when the working of the lighthouse was automated and the keepers, Tony Beswetherick, Jim Losse and Mike Hall, withdrawn. A Telecom land line from Broadstairs, Kent, now monitors the performance of the light.[9]

With automation the crane room became the battery/charger room, the store room the engine room, and the service room was filled with telemetry equipment.

This step meant an end to the assistance of lighthouse keepers in notifying the police and coastguards of climbers stranded on the cliffs, or of falls from the cliff top. At least now ill men did not have to be taken to hospital, as in May 1966 when an injured lighthousekeeper was lifted off by Eastbourne's *Beryl Tollemache* lifeboat, handled with great skill in a rough sea by Coxswain John Bassett.

It also ended the service to the lighthouse of the Friends of the Royal Sovereign Lightship/Beachy Head Lighthouse. Since 1935 they had distributed Christmas food and gifts, donated by local shopkeepers, to the lighthousemen.[10]

The Royal Sovereign is the name of a shoal notorious for shipwrecks before a buoy was sited there in 1850 (see Appendix 3). The shoal was named after a ship, the *Royal Sovereign,* which sailed its trials there in 1637 as the *Sovereign,* being renamed after the Restoration of 1660. Some, however, say it was where a warship called the *Royal Sovereign* was wrecked in 1757.[11]

It wasn't unknown for the lightship, which replaced the buoy in April 1876, to be damaged itself: run down by the Barrow steamer, *Argus,* in April 1888 it had to be replaced with a temporary light until repaired, and was later hit by a 782-ton Panamanian freighter in fog. It was permanently replaced in 1971 by the light-tower which can be seen east of Beachy Head looking like a marine mushroom. The Royal Sovereign achieved stardom more recently in the radio Shipping Forecasts, '...NE by N, force 3, visibility 11 miles, 1003 rising slowly'.

In 1987 Trinity House, following an examination of navigational aids, announced that the future of many lighthouses including Beachy Head was under review. The lighthouse, now with a 880 000 candelas light (equivalent to about a thousand 100W light bulbs) on day and night, costs £15 500 a year to maintain and it could be redundant in these days of electronic navigational aids.

Beacons and bonfires

Beachy Head appears an ideal site for bonfires or beacons for signalling, to spread news, or hold a celebration, and we believe the Romans and Good Queen Bess used it for such purposes. Just over 400 years ago, in July 1588, when the Spanish Armada was first sighted off the tip of Cornwall, the Cornish villagers lit a beacon at the Lizard to send a warning message to the country and this was taken up in Sussex.[12]

Having said that, in the Middle Ages many local bonfires were probably on Willingdon Hill, just inland, where they could be seen from further away.

In more recent times Beachy Head was definitely the site of the beacon for Queen Victoria's Diamond Jubilee, for a 20-ton Jubilee Bonfire on 6 May 1935, kept going by 20 gallons of paraffin oil, and for a popular Coronation Beacon on 2 June 1953.

Apart from the regular burning down of the Beachy Head Hotel (see Chapter 1) there have been other blazes.

The Jubilee Beacon on 6 June 1977 saw Beachy Head's first traffic jam. Over 5000 people poured on to Beachy Head with the intention of seeing Eastbourne's Mayor, Mrs Kathleen Raven, light up as part of the national chain of 103 beacons, fired off by the Queen at Windsor. It was due to be lit at 2215h, but the Mayor, who was half-an-hour late, said, 'I have never seen such traffic chaos. We were fortunate to get to Beachy Head at all. Luckily we met a police car to escort us!' For three hours afterwards all the approach roads were blocked - although this was partly because the beacon burnt out within 30 minutes, so everyone left at once.[13] The network had been organised by the Royal Institute of Chartered Surveyors and locally by Strutt & Parker of Lewes.

Since 1977 there have been beacons or bonfires almost every year and 1981 even saw three. There was one in June for the Festival of Light; one in July to celebrate the wedding of the Prince of Wales (when more than 3000 watched); and on New Year's Eve, when the aim was to promote "Maritime England" as part of the English Tourist Board's publicity campaign.

In 1988 there were celebrations of the 400th anniversary of the defeat of the Spanish Armada. Again, thousands flocked to Beachy Head on Tuesday, 19 July 1988, to take part in an historic occasion; the longest chain of beacons since the Armada, in which 461 were set alight over the length and breadth of the country.

After the fashion of Sir Francis Drake, who finished his game of bowls before tackling the Spanish, Eastbourne's Deputy Mayor, Mr Aubrey Vickers, took his time to light the commemorative beacon. Cheers erupted once the Firle beacon was seen to be alight, and spectators thundered a countdown to the lighting-up time, achieved at 2221h, just eleven minutes after the first beacon had been lit by the Spanish Ambassador and 17 minutes before the last at Berwick-on-Tweed.

Mr David Stevens, chairman of Eastbourne Borough Council's Downland Advisory committee, presented Mr Vickers with a tie spangled with beacons, and there was entertainment by the Polegate Jazz Band, from just north of Eastbourne. However, as soon as the brazier (made by Cavendish Ironworks) was alight, the spectators thinned out and went home.[14]

On a par with the lighthouse for attraction was the beacon to celebrate fifty years of relative peace on the anniversary of the end of World War II, VE-Day, 8 May 1995.

3   SHIPWRECKS and LIFEBOATS

Nowadays, sailing along the coast is a pleasant holiday pastime, and to the satellite-guided skipper out in the Channel the sight of Beachy Head is of little concern. To the coast-hugging mariner of old, however, Beachy Head was a fearsome appearance and its rock ledges and fast running tides were the cause of many disastrous wrecks.[1]

Over 70 shipwrecks are recorded at Beachy Head[2] and undoubtedly there have been more, some marked only by seamen washed ashore, or mentioned solely in dry legal wrangles about the cargo, or in the distant past not remarked upon at all.

Ships have run ashore bereft of crew, who had escaped in the ship's boats thinking the ship was about to go down, and in 1795 there was even a ship which ran aground - when the crew made it safely ashore - only for it to slide out to sea again. The captain didn't give up, he hired a boat, chased his empty ship, and managed to reboard it and bring it safely into Dover.[3]

The earliest name we have is the *Marie* of Santander wrecked in 1368, and we know that some of the crew got ashore.

In 1617 a Dutch ship was wrecked at Burlingate (Birling Gap): a shipwreck known solely because there was an action in the Admiralty Court by the Dutch East India Company for the recovery of its cargo.

The only mark of a wreck in 1676 (Budgen[4] says 1678) is an entry in the Eastbourne Parish Church Register of a burial which states, "A seaman cast ashore at Beachy in a vessel laden with corne". At least five similar entries occur.

Two ships were wrecked at Beachy Head in February 1729. A balance sheet states that an anchor and cable seized as wreck sold for £17, while the expenses of salvage and the burial of three seamen came to £7.50p.

Ten years later the English ship *Apollo* from Barbados to London, laden with sugar, was driven ashore east of Birling Gap, with the Captain and eleven men saved and eight drowned.

All we know of one wreck is contained in a letter (in the Compton Place Muniments, dated 14 January 1741) from Mr Nicholas Gilbert to the Earl of Wilmington. "There being a great number of tubs of butter some tallow and raw beef hides taken up this morning in the Manor of Bourne (which are supposed to be part of the cargo of a ship that was wrecked last night in the Manor of Birling) ... as there is not a Soul Saved out of the Ship's Crew, and as the Hides and Butter will soon Spoyle I should be extremely glad of your Lordship's advice ... "

While we may not know the names of all the wrecks, some are famous, such as the *Nympha Americana* in 1747, which attracted attention because of its rich booty.[5] Cedar-built, of 800 tons and 60-guns it was captured by Commodore George Walker near Cadiz. On passage from Portsmouth to London she was wrecked off Crowlink (some say Birling Gap) on 29 November around 2300h.

She broke asunder amidships and the forepart capsized, drowning 30 out of the 130 crew. The ship's doctor drowned when he attempted to swim ashore. It was said that her cargo consisted of superfine velvets, gold and silver laces, £5000 in money, and £30 000 worth of quicksilver.

Lambert's 1748 engraving of the Nympha Americana *wreck showing pillagers*

The richness of the wreck attracted people from "different parts" and great quantities of her cargo were carried off. It is said 60 persons perished on the beach, one was shot for looting, one died after a fall from the cliff in which he broke his thigh, and the others from an excess of "the Spiritous Liquors they took from the ship", but there is doubt as to the accuracy of these contemporary reports. A Mr Fletcher, Riding Officer, (whom we will meet in the chapter on smuggling) is reported to have recovered a great quantity of money for the owners. Another unlikely story was that two guns from the wreck found their way to Birling Farm.

The story of the maritime nations can be traced by the changes in Beachy Head wrecks and their cargoes, as countries strove for prominence and fortune.

On Monday morning, 1 March 1763 a 32-gun frigate came ashore at Cuckmere in fog, the crew firing guns of distress heard by people at "East Dene", who helped to save the crew of nearly 100. Typical of the ways of the time, it had been a French ship, captured by the British, bought by the East India Company, who let it to the government as a store ship and it was on the way to be laid up.[6]

An episode in the War of American Independence is represented. On Friday morning, 27 November 1778, the *Golden Fleece* was wrecked at Birling Gap. She had sailed from New York on 16 November with 40 passengers on board comprising mainly disabled soldiers from America, including some wounded in the engagement at Freehold Court House. Seven died on the deck, one who leapt from the ship was killed when hit by a mast and other bodies "will be found in the hold", but most escaped.

The following year Nicholas Friend of Crowlink Farm was charged with "...having taken and concealed sundry stones and metals taken from the said wreck

[The *Golden Fleece*]...the Act of Parliament to be read at the...churches of East Dean and Friston...that plundering and robbing such wreck is felony".[7]

The Dutch were coming to the end of their pre-eminence at sea when, in March 1788, a Dutch ship struck the rocks off Crowlink and was dashed to pieces, every soul on board perishing with the exception of one man. "On his getting to land and seeing some people making towards him, he fled from them like a wild man, but being very feeble was soon overtaken and sensible of the friendly intentions of those who followed him, he permitted them to conduct him to the house of Mr Willard of Birling."[8]

One wreck provided a commentary on conditions at sea. On another Friday morning, 23 January 1789, the *Syren,* a West Indiaman, from St Ann's, Jamaica, laden with rum, sugar and pimento, and 15 weeks in passage, was "by the violence of the wind driven on the rocks between Darby's Hole and Beachy Head". All the crew were saved, but the ship became a complete wreck. The crew was so short of provisions that each man's allowance had only been one biscuit a day for the last fortnight and the quantity of fresh water aboard was only 20 gallons. It was reported that only three of the crew were fit for work when the ship struck.[9]

Every combination of loss and survival is found. On 1 November 1790 the brig *Two Brothers* with a cargo of lemons was wrecked at Birling Gap. The crew was saved, but the cargo was lost. Many thousands of lemons were washed ashore and picked up by locals who sold them for two shillings (10p) per 100. Conversely, the *Charming Sally,* laden with corn, was wrecked at Birling Gap in January 1796, and all on board perished, but the cargo was saved.

The same year, the *Ann Amelia,* a Swedish galliot, *en route* from Bordeaux to Lübeck with wine, was wrecked at Birling Gap on 10 May. The crew was saved, but the ship became a total loss. Two days later soldiers from the Eastbourne Barracks who were helping to unload the wreck, got a taste of the wine by catching it in their caps and shoes as it ran from the seams of the vessel. "They would soon have been troublesome and mischievous had they not been prevented by the arrival of a sergeant's guard who compelled them to quit the wreck and return to their barracks."[10] In other words, back to waiting for "Boney".

Yet another cargo gets a mention when on 4 January 1798 a ship belonging to the South Sea Whale Fishery, with butts of blubber aboard, was stranded off Beachy Head. The crew was saved.

People had always striven to help shipwrecked seamen in one way or another, although their efforts did not make much impact and the wrecks continued. On 2 February 1807 the *Margaret,* with a cargo of slate, was driven ashore at the Gap.

James Royer's Eastbourne Guide Book[11] of 1799 says, under the heading Berling Gap, "Mr Willard has in his possession an iron cage for saving as such as may be shipwrecked under those immense perpendicular cliffs near the Gap, so contrived by windlasses and pullies etc by capstans fastened in the ground, so as to draw up the cage, which holds five or six persons at a time." The apparatus consisted of a two-wheeled trolley that could be drawn to the cliff edge, securely fixed, and a rope run over pulleys to let down the birdcage-like basket so that the mariners could climb in and be hauled up. There is no evidence that Mr Willard's contraption ever saved a life from the beach, and the appalling loss of ships and lives each winter

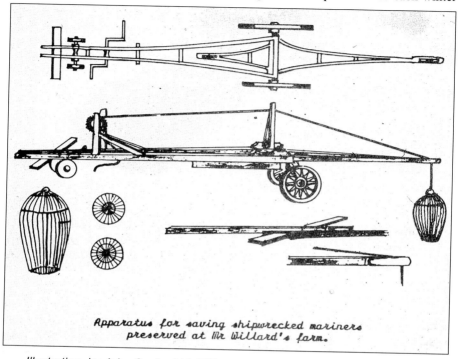

Apparatus for saving shipwrecked mariners preserved at Mr Willard's farm.

Illustration, by John Cant, of Mr Willard's apparatus for saving shipwrecked mariners {from a portfolio of watercolours by Francis Grose in Hastings Museum}

remained unchecked until lifeboats were introduced and the Belle Tout light came on in 1828.

The Willard referred to was Nicholas Willard, who continued to occupy Birling Manor after it was sold to Charles Gilbert about 1808.[12]

Lifeboats

A system of boats ready for emergencies, manned by local volunteers, was an early concerted attempt to save seamen in distress. The first lifeboats along this stretch of coast were at Rye and Newhaven in 1803.[13] Next in line, a lifeboat station was established at Eastbourne in 1822.[14] Its first lifeboat, a 25-foot rowing boat, provided by John Fuller MP of Rose Hill, was in service 1822-63. Some say it was called the *Good Samaritan,* others that it had no name.

On 4 March 1824 the National Institution for Preservation of Life from Shipwreck was founded, which in 1854 changed its name to the Royal National

Lifeboat Institution (RNLI). The Newhaven lifeboat base was established on the west bank of the Ouse River in 1824 shortly after the Institution was formed.

The official Eastbourne lifeboat was soon in operation, covering the "patch" of Birling Gap to Bexhill. When the *Isabella,* a Dutch East Indiaman, was wrecked off Eastbourne, in February 1833, the lifeboat made two trips to take off 29 of the crew. John Fuller had a medal struck to commemorate the occasion. As a former MP he was aware of the value of publicity, for the medal bore his portrait.

In December 1845 another Dutch East Indiaman, the *Twee Cornelisson,* was wrecked off Eastbourne. All 28 crew were rescued by the *Good Samaritan.*

Eastbourne's first lifeboat was replaced by the 33-foot *Mary Stirling,* another sailing boat with ten oars. She was only launched five times over 17 years' service.

Shortly after the *Livonia* sank following a collision off Beachy Head, on 23 January 1875, its captain, swept by the sea near Eastbourne's lifeboat station, was brought ashore. His wants were attended to by Samuel Place, local agent of the Shipwrecked Mariners' Aid Society, another of the groups helping sailors.[15]

Five days later the *Dunmore* ran aground at Pevensey. Anchors were put down with the assistance of coastguards and the lifeboat, and later she refloated. For their part in the rescue the lifeboat crew were subsequently awarded £300.

After the *Rubens* was saved the next year, some Eastbourne fishermen entered a High Court action to recover salvage money. George Hide and his crew were awarded £237, John Allchorn £75 and James Swain £55.[16]

Not all rescue attempts were successful. On Thursday night, 7 September 1876, the Eastbourne lifeboat put out to the assistance of a large brig or schooner that sank about 1½ miles off the Belle Tout cliffs, but was unable to find any sign of the ship or survivors.

The *William and Mary,* another self-righting sailing boat with ten oars, was the lifeboat from 1880 to 1899. It took part in the most sensational launch of an Eastbourne lifeboat, when the 480-ton Norwegian barque *New Brunswick,* on way from Quebec to Sunderland, got into difficulties near Belle Tout.

By dawn on Sunday, 25 November 1883, the *New Brunswick's* topmasts had been carried away and with her sails torn to rags she was being carried by a SSW gale towards the Beachy Head rocks. Two anchors were put out, but on finding they were dragging, the crew hoisted signals of distress.

On shore the signals were seen, but the Newhaven lifeboat was unable to leave harbour, and the heavy weather and wind direction meant there were doubts whether the Eastbourne lifeboat could be launched. Councillor Thomas Bennett and Alderman Rudd, Lloyd's agents, Mr HM Emary, local Honorary Secretary of the RNLI, and Charles Hide, Coxswain of the lifeboat, decided that in the prevailing weather it was not possible to sail west from Eastbourne, and the only way to reach the *New Brunswick* was to launch the lifeboat from Birling Gap.

Plenty of help was forthcoming and the *William and Mary* lifeboat was pulled by hand on its wheeled carriage as far as South Street before the first team of six horses could be harnessed - increased to ten horses for the steep ascent of the newly constructed Duke's Drive. Some of the roads were not in as good condition as to-day and at one point the only way was across ploughed fields.

The difficulties were not over on reaching the Gap. The cutting to the beach was too narrow for the carriage wheels to pass and the rough seas had washed away the lower eight feet of the slope. An impromptu slipway was made from timber by willing hands and the lifeboat was launched, but the storm was so violent that it took over an hour to reach the *New Brunswick,* only a mile away. Once alongside a rope was made fast and the crew taken off one by one, until all were saved with only one injured.

By now the barque's anchors were holding, and as the storm subsided the Newhaven tug was able to bring the *New Brunswick* safely into port. Charlie "Bones" Hide, the Coxswain, was a local hero, but an unfortunate sequel was that "Bones" and other members of the crew made a claim for life salvage of the ship, in contravention of RNLI rules. The argument dragged on with ill-feeling on both sides, an untidy ending for what was undoubtedly a supremely brave rescue. Mr Emary's sketches of the rescue are in the Towner Art Gallery.[17]

The collier *Tally Ho,* of 189 tons, was wrecked on Boxing Day, 1886. It sprang a leak in a gale off Beachy Head so the captain ran the ship ashore at Eastbourne, but in the raging surf three of the crew of seven died. Eastbourne did not have a rocket apparatus at the time and the light marking the fishermen's quarters had blown out. A line was got aboard, but one seaman died when he failed to pull in the rope, jumped too soon and was lost in the darkness. At the inquest the view was that all the crew would have been saved if a rocket apparatus had been available. It has to be said that many colliers were unseaworthy old tubs - four Sussex colliers appeared in Samuel Plimsoll's "black list".[18]

The first portent of to-day's massive tankers was in 1887 when the *Sjødronningan* of 850-tons with a cargo of petroleum went ashore off Belle Tout on 4 January. The Eastbourne lifeboat under Coxswain Huggett saved the crew.

In 1899 the *William and Mary* lifeboat was replaced by the *James Stevens No 6* (1899-1924) assisted by the *Olive* (1903-21). Both were sailing boats with oars.

By a coincidence the very ship that laid the cross-Channel cable from Birling Gap was responsible for severing it. The 1004-ton, twin screw steamer *International* drifted ashore at Birling Gap on Saturday, 30 September 1899.

Built at Stockton-on-Tees in 1870, she had been in the service of the India Rubber and Gutta Percha and Telegraph Works of London. Sold to a French company, she was on tow to Cherbourg when she broke loose from the tug in heavy seas and came ashore broadside on. The Newhaven lifeboat took off all the crew, and she later broke up.

Although the wreck of the *Peruvian* in February 1899 was off Seaford, not Beachy Head, and the life boat was not involved in her rescue, she was the making of a legend on the local beaches. Her cargo was ivory and logwood, the ivory in the form of "ivory nuts" (about the size of beach pebbles) used for making buttons. The crew, including the Captain's dog, were saved by rocket apparatus, but she broke up with scarcely anything left of the vessel, except the ivory nuts which were everywhere. It was said they were thickly strewn at Cuckmere Haven, and could be picked up under the Seven Sisters into the 1970s.

The ss International *aground at Birling Gap, 1899 {Reeves, Lewes}*

The *Caroline,* with a cargo of 140 tons of coal, was driven ashore near Eastbourne in August 1900. The crew stayed on board in the hope that they could get off at high water. The conditions became worse and the lifeboat was brought from the Terriss Memorial Lifeboat House and launched, watched by several thousand spectators. The crew, including the captain (who had elected to stay with the *Caroline* initially) were saved by rocket apparatus.

For a 1902 launch in a full gale the midship oars were double-banked.

The new lighthouse didn't stop all the strandings. On Saturday 14 May 1904 the *Emma Louise,* a German schooner, ran ashore in dense fog 200m west of the lighthouse. A rocket was fired from the cliff, but the crew was unable to secure the rope and the Newhaven lifeboat took them off. Later the ship was refloated.[19]

Eastbourne's first motorised lifeboat was the *Priscilla Macbean* (1921-27), although like its replacement, the *LP & St Helen* (1927-29), it had sails.[20] During a 1925 launch bowman Harry Hendy was injured and never fully recovered.

The next Eastbourne lifeboat, the *Jane Holland,* did rescue a seaman on 1 June 1930, but 14 lives were lost when the Swedish steamer *Inger* sank after a collision near the Royal Sovereign. Conditions were bad with a visibility of 30m.

There was some criticism of the time taken to launch the Eastbourne lifeboat in February 1936 when the *Davenport* sprang a leak off Beachy Head and came ashore. Her signals had not been seen at first and the tide was low, so the ship's decks were awash, with the seamen clinging to the rigging before, at first light, the lifeboat went out to save all the crew and two pet dogs.[21]

The first lifeboat episode of the Second World War was on 20 March 1940 when the 5430-ton *Barnhill,* was bombed off Beachy Head by a German bomber and set on fire. Four seamen died in the attack and others were missing, but the Jane Holland brought back 28 of the crew, although one died later that day. Later the ship's bell was heard from ashore so the lifeboatmen put out again, with Dr DG Churcher aboard. They found that the ship's captain, grievously injured when blown off the bridge, had managed to crawl back and grip the bell rope with his teeth. He was taken to hospital and lived to visit the town a year later. The two lifeboatmen who braved red-hot plates to board the burning and drifting ship, Alec Huggett and Thomas Allchorn, received the RNLI bronze medal.

The James Stevens No 6 *lifeboat outside the lifeboat house, now the museum*

The *Jane Holland* next went to Dunkirk in June 1940, where she was rammed, hit by 500 bullets, and finally abandoned off the French coast. Two days later she was found in the Channel, towed to Dover and after a refit returned to Eastbourne.

In 1949 she was replaced by the 41-foot *Beryl Tollemache,* the gift of Sir Lyonel and Lady Tollemache. Its first rescue, off Cow Gap, was of two children whose canoe had capsized. They were rushed to hospital, but both died.

The stranding of the *Germania* near Cow Gap after a collision has already been mentioned. She came aground in dense fog on 26 April 1955, half-a-mile east of the lighthouse. When news reached the Eastbourne lifeboat it put out and landed 23 of the crew, but the captain and others remained on board. On 6 May 1955 huge waves forced the rescue of 16 men left aboard. This was a difficult rescue, amid rocks, and Coxswain Allchorn was awarded his second RNLI bronze medal, and mechanic Michael Hardy a citation on vellum.

Every type of emergency is attended. When a Greek freighter, the *Aghios Georgios II*, caught fire off Eastbourne on 30 April 1963, the captain, his wife and crew of 16 were taken to Eastbourne by the lifeboat.

The first inflatable in-shore boat, a D-class, was stationed at Eastbourne in 1964. The maximum speed, about 20 knots, and later up to 27 knots (30mph) was much faster than the larger vessels, and it could manoeuvre close inshore. These boats are ideal for rescues of small dinghies and swimmers, and in the last 30 years have been launched over 300 times.

On 13 September 1964, the *Beryl Tollemache* lifeboat rescued two young men from a waterlogged 50-footer in rough seas off Beachy Head. The next year it took 27 off the Greek ship *Nymfea* in fog, and on 8 January 1967 rescued 14 crew and a passenger from the East German cargo vessel *Saale* on fire following a collision.

Various vessels took the crew off the tanker, *Sitakund,* after explosions in the Channel at 1900h on Sunday 20 October 1968. On the Monday she came to rest less than a mile off Holywell, although there was a further explosion on the Tuesday.[22] The lifeboat, under Coxswain Derek Huggett, assisted the Eastbourne Fire Brigade as it fought the flames.

On 29 July 1972 the lifeboat searched all night for a missing Swedish boat without success - it had managed to limp into Shoreham.

As a sign of changing times, on 17 November 1973, a helicopter landed firemen to help fight a fire on the German cargo ship, *Cap San Antonio.*

On more routine duties the Eastbourne lifeboat was called out on 20 October 1974, when the *Jean B* sprang a leak off Beachy Head, and when the *Wittering,* a British coaster, collided with a German container ship in the afternoon of 24 February 1976. On this occasion both the Eastbourne and Hastings lifeboats stood by, along with an RAF helicopter, and when the *Wittering* started to sink by the bow the Hastings lifeboat took off the crew.[23]

In 1977 *Beryl Tollemache* was replaced by the *Charles Dibdin.* Sometimes lifeboats from another station are temporarily assigned, which was the case with the *Charles Dibdin*, replaced two years later by the *Duke of Kent,* a new Rother class boat 37 feet long with a speed of 8 knots.

Neither of the lifeboats are used routinely for cliff rescues, although on occasions they have stood off in case their help was needed. If there is injury or access is difficult, immediate transportation to hospital, now possible under almost all conditions by helicopter, is clearly in the rescued person's favour (see Cliff Rescues, Chapter 5). After an explosion on a ship off Beachy Head in February 1983 an injured seaman was airlifted directly to hospital.

Lifeboats are still necessary and the tradition of the local sailors continues. For a 1902 launch, eight members of the Erridge family were in the boat, and in December 1983 three Eastbourne lifeboatmen were presented with bravery awards for rescuing a woman and two children whose dinghy had capsized. The in-shore boat was used in 1979 to take off four people stranded by the tide at the foot of Beachy Head, and in 1988 to recover the body of a 77-year-old man, floating amid rocks below Devil's Chimney. In November 1989 both lifeboats were involved in a recovery near Belle Tout after a 30-year-old drove his van over the cliff. Lifeboat Coxswain Graham Cole said the inshore boat retrieved the body from the semi-submerged van and passed it to the offshore boat, the *Duke of Kent,* which had put out from Langney Point to help.[24]

By 1990 the Eastbourne lifeboat had been launched about 500 times and saved some 500 persons. During 1996, when lifeboats round the coasts of Britain saved nearly 1000 lives, the Eastbourne lifeboats were launched over 100 times for the third year running. The off-shore boat, now the *Royal Thames* (one of a breed of much faster lifeboats) was launched on 68 occasions, with 47 for the in-shore boat, the *Humphry and Nora Tollemache II.* The biggest rescue involved the Swedish bulk carrier *Lidan,* on fire off Beachy Head in August, but over the year under Coxswain Dave Corke 200 people were helped and 18 lives saved, from sinking motor cruisers, to windsurfers, and pranksters jumping off the pier.[25]

The Lifeboat Museum, Eastbourne

The first official lifeboat station was built near Marine Road in 1857, but just to the east of the Wish Tower is a rectangular red-brick building which was the lifeboat house and is now a Lifeboat Museum.

The foundation stone of this lifeboat house was laid by the Duchess of Devonshire on 16 July 1898. Named after William Terriss, an actor murdered in 1897, who had a love of the sea and an affection for the town, the £1314 cost was met by public subscription. The building acted as a lifeboat house from 1898 to 1924, when it was used to house the *James Stevens No 6* as a exhibition boat.

A second boathouse, of corrugated iron and costing £445, opened near the Fishing Station in 1902. It was used by the *Olive* in the summer with the *James Stevens No 6* at the Terriss Boathouse. They reversed positions over the year.

On 22 March 1937 Sir Godfrey Baring, chairman of the RNLI, opened the Terriss Boathouse as the first lifeboat museum in the UK; Lady Seymour Hicks, daughter of Terriss, was in attendance. Mrs Astley Roberts, chairman of the Eastbourne Ladies' Lifeboat Guild and wife of a local GP, donated the clock on the roof. The building closed during the 1939-45 war, but opened again as a lifeboat museum in 1947. The clock was replaced in 1971.

When the museum opened the *James Stevens No 6* was sold to Allchorn Bros for "trips round the bay". In 1940 it went to France to help evacuate the BEF.

From 1924 all the lifeboats were housed at the Fishing Station, Royal Parade, east of the pier, until in 1994 the lifeboat base was moved to the outer basin of the new Marina, near Langney.

4   COASTGUARDS, SIGNALS and SMUGGLING

Coastal trading has taken place from the Eastbourne beach for hundreds of years, and probably since Roman times. For the purposes of combating smuggling Sussex was divided into five areas: in 1680 the Rye area extended from Camber to Beachy Head. Shortly afterwards the Customs and Excise were administered separately. Customs officials were present at Sea Houses, Eastbourne, based near the Ordnance Yard working alongside Excise officials, who probably used the warehouse known to have stood in Church Street on the site of Edgmond Hall.

They were also involved when ships carrying cargoes of taxable goods were wrecked. In April 1735 a boat from France to Lübeck was drawn by the tide against Beachy Head, but the captain and crew managed to save their lives. The Customs Officers took charge of the cargo of 150 hogsheads of wine. Not so lucky were the crew of a Dutch ship bound for Cadiz from Amsterdam which foundered in November the following year. The mate and eleven men were saved, but the captain and eight of his crew drowned. Upwards of 20 000 crowns in Spanish coin were saved by the Bourne Custom Officer and carried by soldiers to the Newhaven Custom House.

A series of organisations was set up to combat the smuggling which had increased in Napoleonic times. The Preventive Waterguard, an inshore force, manned by the Royal Navy, was introduced in 1809 to support the Customs and Excise Services in the control of smuggling. They had a presence at Eastbourne, but in 1818 the Preventive Waterguard was superseded by the Coast Blockade for the prevention of smuggling.

The Coast Blockade was a naval force introduced expressly to combat the increase in smuggling. Stations were established along the Kent and Sussex coast extending west to Seaford Head. The Coast Blockade moved into Eastbourne in 1819 and had four stations between Beachy Head and Fairlight as part of a signalling chain. The force was extended to cover the entire Sussex coast in 1824.

The Eastbourne Watch House was built for the Coast Blockade on the shingle near a corner of the Ordnance Yard, along with a warehouse and boathouse.

Saving life at sea was one of the Coast Blockade's functions and in November 1824 when the *Juno* was wrecked at Birling Gap, the Master, Francis Le Fevre and his crew of five were rescued by Lieutenant Joseph Clark RN and a crew of eight from the Coast Blockade. Lt Clark was awarded a gold medal and each of his crew received two gold sovereigns.[1]

Coastguard Service

This service was established in 1822. The Coast Blockade was abolished in 1831, and in March of that year the Coastguards took over the preventive work, life saving and other duties along the Kent and Sussex coast.

The work of the coastguards always included cliff and sea rescues, signalling and observation. They had a responsibility for wreckage as well; for example, following a collision in the Channel in September 1879, items from one of the ships - the oars, the long boat and timber - were collected up from the beach by the coastguards and auctioned.

They also kept up the tradition of assisting ships in distress. When the *Fairfax* went ashore east of Crowlink in February 1881, the coastguards lowered a rope ladder "kept for such a purpose" and rescued the crew.

Initially coastguard stations were established at Martello Towers 53, 55, 57, and 62, at Langney Fort East, at Holywell (Meads), Birling Gap, Crowlink and Cuckmere Haven.

The Watch House was used as accommodation for the Chief Coastguard Officer and his family. After a storm in 1857 it became unusable so this station was removed to nearby Hurst's Cottages, Seaside, and later to Addingham Road.

Cottages for the coastguards were erected in Latimer Road and Wartling Road, Eastbourne, while Meads, Beachy Head, Birling Gap, Crowlink and Cuckmere Haven each had a row of coastguard cottages.

The Eastbourne Census for 1841 shows that seven families lived at the Meads station.[2] It was the custom to move coastguards around, to stop collusion, and only two were born in Sussex. Beachy Head station also had seven coastguards, Jos Harrison, Ben Kerrye, Will Studley, Will Tully, Ted Earl, GF Saunders and J Muir, none of whom had been born in Sussex. The Eastbourne Rate Book of the time mentions houses at Beachy Head owned by the Board of Customs, with a reference to them being built by Edward Maynard, a local builder.

The Crowlink coastguard station was beyond the end of the farm road, by the Seven Sisters cliffs,[3] in the 1830s three coastguard families lived there. The coastguard hut at Crowlink fell into the sea around 1900, but there was a small look-out on Flagstaff Brow (see Chapter 10) during 1914-18. The three cottages closed in 1921 and both cottages and look-out were destroyed in the 1939-45 war.

The siting and importance of these stations altered during the 19th century. The Meads coastguard station was not in use after the 1870s, and the Beachy Head station, hitherto a detachment of Birling Gap, took over in strategic importance. In 1890 St Luke's Hospital for children was opened on the Meads station site, and it is now occupied by the *Dolphin Court* flats.

The boat house, rocket house and watch room of Birling Gap coastguard station have long since fallen into the sea (see Chapter 1) along with part of the coastguard cottages. A lookout on the hill towards Belle Tout was built in the 19th century, but had to be demolished after the 1939-45 war. It was replaced by a two-storey building, manned on-call by six part-timers, and in turn this was demolished in the early 1990s. The auxiliaries could be called upon by a maroon fired near East Dean village for cliff rescue and life-saving by breeches-buoy.[4]

Coast life-saving gear is now in the hut at the north end of the row of coastguard cottages. A trailer is kept loaded at all times, but the breeches-buoy went in 1982 with more reliance on helicopters. There is an inflatable boat housed to the west of the hotel by the Birling Gap Safety Boat Association, to keep watch for any swimming and boating accidents at the Gap.

Signal Stations

Beachy Head has been used for signalling purposes over the centuries, and as mentioned, it was one of a chain of fire beacons lit in times of peril. In 1795 a system of permanent signal stations, manned by naval personnel, was set up along the coast. A painting in the Towner Art Gallery, dating from 1800, shows a view of Beachy Head from the sea, with an indication of a flagstaff on the cliff top.

By 1803 there were ten stations in Sussex, from West Wittering to Fairlight, and including Beachy Head and Seaford. Each station was armed with a gun, usually a 12-pounder, and the name "Gun Gardens" may have arisen from this association. The flagstaffs were 50 feet high and the semaphore system consisted of a combination of a red flag, a blue pennant, and four balls made of painted black canvas stretched over hoops, which were 3 feet 4 inches in diameter.[5] It was said that a message such as "The French are landing at Hythe" could be passed from the Sussex coast to London within 15 minutes.

The Eastbourne Tithe Map of 1842 marks a strip of land near the cliff top used as a Signal Station, providing further evidence that the signal post had become part of the coastguard system.

Parry, writing in the 1820s, describes Beachy Head, "On one of the extreme heights is a Signal Station, with a flagstaff and two or three guns". Some early editions of the OS one-inch-to-the-mile maps, dating from 1813, show a square building on Beachy Head marked "Signal" which might have been part of the Admiralty semaphore station, linked to Deal.[6] The second volume of the Victoria County History in 1907 refers to "...temporary small batteries were thrown up at Beachy Head and Seaford...". It is possible that the position of the Signal Station gun was just below the Coastguard Station as the coastguards took over the original site and in a description of the original coastguard station mention is made of a "small wooden building near to the flagstaff".

The Belle Tout mound was also used for signalling in the Napoleonic War.

The *Sussex County Magazine* says that a little wooden hut on the Beachy Head Downs was intended for a telegraphic station "when an invasion of England by that arch-hypocrite Napoleon III was deemed not improbable".[7]

Lloyd's Watch Tower

Between 1877 and 1904 Lloyd's of London set up a semaphore signalling station here to provide early news of returning ships - information well worth having for both the insurance and commodity markets. A Watch Tower, leased by Lloyd's from the Duke of Devonshire in 1882, was rebuilt by Lloyd's in 1896 and purchased by them the following year. It formed part of their signalling station at Beachy Head until 1904, when the work was transferred to the adjoining naval station, and this arrangement continued into the 1930s. Wireless telegraphy started in 1902 when the coastguards were trained as operators and they provided valuable service in the 1914-18 war. After 1898 the coastguard station also had arrangements with the Meteorological Office to hoist storm signals. The now demolished Signalman's Cottage is described in Chapter 1.

Looking east along the cliff top c. 1910, l-r, the Beachy Head Hotel, the coastguard cottages and Watch Tower, behind its mast {Towner Museum}

Between the wars, when the Watch Tower was no longer needed for its original purpose, it was transformed into a kiosk selling postcards to holidaymakers. The octagonal building was lantern-shaped with a weathervane on the roof, and each of the eight walls had a window. Postcards (some of which showed the semaphore masts) could be sent from the kiosk and bore the cachets "Watch Tower, Beachy Head" within a double-line diamond (1920), or an oval (1935). This correspondence was sent *en masse* to the Eastbourne sorting office and cancelled there in the usual way.

Having been rendered obsolescent, and in a state of disrepair after the war, the Watch Tower was accepted as a gift by the Council in 1948. They tidied it up by removal of the structure above the windowsills. The base now consisted of 12 courses of brick with one side wall left open for access to a penny-in-the-slot telescope with splendid views in all directions. On 25 November 1967 a cliff top seat at the reconstructed Watch Tower was unveiled. A few metres from the walls you can still see the concrete bases for the chains which supported the masts. Two tablets were set in the side of the Watch Tower, one records its use by Lloyd's as a signal station, and the other, dated 1949, records those units from the Corps of Signals based in the area during World War II.

Beachy Head was also used in connection with a triangulation survey prior to the production of Ordnance Survey maps. The *Sussex Weekly Advertiser* of 8 April 1793 noted that a general survey of the Kingdom was being carried out under the direction of the Master General of Ordnance, with use of several stations along the coast including Beachy Head. These activities began in 1782 when Charles Lennox, 3rd Duke of Richmond (1735-1806), was appointed to the post of Master General of the Board of Ordnance. In 1784-7 General William Roy (1726-90) initiated a national survey based on triangulation using "white lights", such as Bengal or Argand lights. This operation was also intended to help with the selection of suitable sites for the signal stations.

Postal cachets of the Watch Tower, Beachy Head

In 1791 Lennox promoted a continuation of the trigonometric survey which led to the Ordnance Survey one-inch-to-the-mile maps of Britain. The first OS map of Sussex was published between 1810 and 1819 in six sheets.

Beachy Head was represented in a later form of signalling. The coastguards were the first national service to have telephones, installed locally in 1892. The National Telephone Company's exchange was connected with the Eastbourne Post Office in 1894. The same year a telegraph office was opened at the Beachy Head Hotel, and two years later was open for business on Sundays.[8] It closed in 1904.

A form of signalling is still practised from Beachy Head as the police operate a radio aerial from near the spot where the coastguards had their station 200 years ago.

Smuggling

Smuggling in Sussex on any scale dates back to the time of Queen Anne. The goods involved were chiefly brandy, tobacco, tea, wine and fine silk.[9]

In the 18th century it was estimated that four million gallons of Dutch gin and five million pounds of tea were smuggled in from France every year, and that two-thirds of all tobacco smoked was smuggled.

Every Sussex beach has tales of smuggling days past, and even present, with the Customs finding drugs in a catamaran at Eastbourne Marina in January 1995. Probably the home of the art was the Crowlink valley where the lonely coast gave access to country whose hills and winding ways might seem providentially constructed for the purpose.

The *Sussex Weekly Advertiser* of 2 December 1776 informs us that Revenue Officers seized upwards of 17 cwt of tea and 9 casks of Geneva (shortened to gin, but derived from juniper) near Friston Mill. Friston is just inland from Crowlink.

The cliffs of Beachy Head were not suitable for landing contraband, but could be used for storage. According to a fictional account by Horace Hutchinson, Parson Darby's successor was much more popular because he was a smuggler.[10]

Around 1800 smuggling was rife and many of the populace, including the fishermen, were ready to take a chance to help themselves. It was decidedly chancy for the fishermen because if caught the penalty was to have their boat cut in half, to prevent further smuggling, and thus they were deprived of their livelihood. To reduce the chances of identification by the Excisemen they adopted nicknames, such as "Catseyes", which persisted for many years.

The "Landers" were violent and ruthless men. They faced execution or transportation if caught, although juries seldom convicted. Friston churchyard has the tomb of Exciseman Thomas Fletcher. The inscription is not easy to make out but it reads,

"...late of this parish and of Seaford port,
June 8th 1750, aged 34".

The story is that one moonless night he was tracking a gang of smugglers along the cliff top where they had placed white chalky stones to delineate the edge. When they realised he was following they moved the stones to lead over the edge with the result that in the dark Fletcher slipped. He managed, however, to hang on to the cliff edge with his fingers, until one of the smugglers returned and stamped on his hands, sending the Exciseman to his death on the beach below.

Accounts exist of smuggling at Birling Gap, chiefly of spirits - gin and brandy. In July 1828 a run of smuggled goods took place there when 37 tubs were landed by the smugglers. They got 25 away, but an alarm was raised by their sentries, so the smugglers allowed 12 tubs to drop to the cliff bottom.

On another occasion 300 smugglers went to Crowlink to load a cargo, but were halted by a sentinel signal. Four nights later they landed 300 half-ankers (a 4-gallon cask) at Seaford. Crowlink had a slipway to the beach until the end of the 19th century, and it was so well used that in London the term "Crowlink" applied to a type of gin. It was said that "Crow Link" coastguards, Mark Johnstone, John Hurdwick and Gordon McNaish, were responsible for apprehending a leading smuggler, "Blinker" Eldridge, at Rough Brow in the 1830s.

Stanton Collins, from the Market Cross Inn, Alfriston, who married a Gorringe, was the leader of the main gang of smugglers. He was finally brought within the law for sheep stealing and sentenced to seven years in Australia. Bob Hall, who died in the Eastbourne workhouse, aged 94, in 1895, was the last surviving member of the gang.[11]

In this vicinity the last open fight between smugglers and coastguards was said to be in January 1833. George Pett, a Coastguard boatman, who was shot by smugglers during the affray, is buried in the parish churchyard at Eastbourne.

Local Coastguards to-day

As taxes changed, the incentive for smuggling lessened and, until the drugs culture, illegal immigrants, and beer-running of the last few decades, little organised smuggling was seen along the coast, but rescues were always needed.

Throughout the 20th century the Coastguard Service has been reorganised, modernised and reduced as technology has developed.[12] When the Birling Gap lookout was closed down in 1951, Senior Officer WT Maynard said, 'I used to have a full-time staff of two and kept watch all night'.[13] Four auxiliaries from East Dean took over, with Mr Ivan Worsell in charge.

In the course of the 1960s an artistic colony started up at the old coastguard cottages, now *Crangon Cottages*. Friends visited resident Rebecca Betts (Dame Barbara Castle's mother) and decided to rent or buy one of the old cottages. Living there by 1994 were daughter-in-law Joyce Betts, Jean Cooke, wife of the painter John Bratby, Betty Lazareno, Jean Fawbert, and Lord Howie of Troon.[14]

Eastbourne had two full-time coastguards in 1973, Garry Russell and Phil Thornton (not replaced when they retired), and 21 auxiliaries; now the numbers are down to 12 and would possibly be less if it were not for the cliff rescue work.

The East Sussex coast to Beachy Head comes under the Dover District. An auxiliary company, under John Wicking, is located in the Eastbourne area, their work organised from Hastings, with Bob Merson in charge. Birling Gap is under Solent and has many of the village families in its ranks, with names such as Bailey, Breach, Eve, Fear, Fuller, Johnson, Taylor and Vine. George Booth-Clibborn only retired in 1996, John Dann still takes part in the patrols after 37 years' part-time service, and Richard Worsell was awarded the MBE in 1997.

5 CLIFF RESCUES AND RECOVERIES

Those who face the task of recovering the victims of "that yawning precipice" Beachy Head, encounter fearsome risks. The many projections bump the rescuer against the cliff face, gashing him on the rows of sharp flints, especially during the haul up. Cuts and abrasions, which often become infected, and bruises from loosened chunks of disintegrating cliff are all in the job. Until recent years there was the added danger of the rope fraying as it rubbed over the jagged cliffs.

The responsibility for rescues and recoveries was in the hands of the police for a long time and bravely did they discharge their duties without the benefit of modern rescue aids. Others played a part; on 26 December 1946, RSPCA Inspector Winn went down 100m to rescue a puppy. The local Fire Brigade performed the task for five years, but for over 20 years from October 1973 the Coastguard Service (always associated with helping those stranded round our coasts) assumed the responsibilities, and still plays a part to-day. It so happens that policemen and firemen, along with many other trades and professions, are represented among the volunteer rescuers. Auxiliaries for a typical 1980s' recovery operation would be two fishermen, two employees of the Dental Practice Board, two from Seeboard, a taximan and two who were otherwise unemployed.

Parts of the cliff are more treacherous than others, but with the risk of falling rubble ever present, the coastguards routinely wear safety helmets and protective clothing to withstand the buffeting.

The coastguard-in-charge, Garry Russell, was injured on 15 May 1980 during an attempt to recover a 43-year-old Brighton woman from her wrecked car, which she had driven over near the old Belle Tout lighthouse.[1] Pieces of rock fell on his legs, requiring hospital attention, yet following treatment he returned to the scene. After a previous rock fall incident he was off work for 13 weeks, and he has twice suffered a badly infected hand.

The manner of rescue is determined by the circumstances, although helicopters are used more and more. Sometimes the victims are lowered to the beach; usually, however, they are brought up to the top because respectful transportation of the stretcher along the boulder-strewn beach takes time, apart from the hazards of tide and spray. In 1967 a woman was carried, by four policemen, from west of the lighthouse to a police van at Whitbread Hollow, by way of Cow Gap. One of the four described, in typical understatement, the one-and-three-quarter mile slog as, 'A very difficult journey, even though helped by Mr CR Saunders, ...walking through an incoming tide on occasions up to our knees in water'.

For many years the rule was to lower the rescuer at the end of a rope to the spot, where he untied his rope and affixed it to the victim. After a signal to his colleagues above, the body would be carefully drawn up the cliffs with the rescuer remaining on the beach, or a handy ledge, until the rope was lowered again.

Exceptionally, it was necessary for the helpers to pull up the rescuer at the same time to allow him to protect the injured or unconscious person from further hurt.

The routine was that if someone fell over, or there was a report that someone was trapped on a ledge, or if there was other evidence such as an abandoned car, the police alerted the coastguard officer-in-charge who notified the volunteer helpers by means of the Fairlight (Hastings) Coastguard Station. The coastguards hitch up the ready-packed rescue trailer, housed near the Beachy Head Hotel, and drive to the scene. By the way, if you ever need to call the coastguards dial 999.

The heavy, slow tripod mechanism used to lower the Police down the cliff in the 1960s. PC Ward's "tin hat" lies on the ground {Towner Museum}

Apart from the coastguard-in-charge, there used to be over 20 local men who volunteered to help in rescues. Any call-out team consists of one or two cliff rescuemen along with half-a-dozen assistant coastguards plus, for power and transport, a Land Rover and trailer. The Land Rover has a power-driven capstan on the front bumper, and the trailer carries two nylon ropes, a main line about 375m (1200 ft) long and a safety line also 1200 feet, at least at the start of its existence. To allow for the irregularity of the slopes, almost 700 feet of rope is needed to reach the beach at Gun Gardens - one of the highest parts.

The coastguards choose the most suitable site above the incident and the Land Rover is stationed about 15m from the cliff edge, facing the sea.

Two assistants don harness belts (which have a rope attached) and each secure their rope to a metal peg, knocked into the turf, about three metres from the cliff edge. They then work on the very edge of the cliff to erect the tubular aluminium derrick. The two side limbs, each some 12 feet (4m) long, are staked into the cliff top about five feet apart and as near to the edge as possible, so that the apex can lean over the edge. The middle limb is directed landwards from the apex and is kept supported by wires attached to a series of pegs. The rescuers previously had heavy metal tripods, which needed three men to lift, but Mr Russell introduced alloy (which could be carried by one man) and when he changed the design from a three-leg tripod to a two-leg derrick it was the first of its type in Britain.

The main line starts from the bin in the trailer, runs round the Land Rover capstan, goes towards the cliff and over a running wheel to the pulley blocks which are attached in the apex of the derrick. Garry Russell resolved not to have any hand winch, which required three turns for every few feet, and had just two gears - "slow and almost imperceptible". The safety line, played out by two assistants, runs from the trailer around a metal peg and again over a running wheel to the derrick.

Garry Russell guides the rescueman and assistants on the cliff edge

The cliff rescueman routinely dons safety harness, helmet, distinctive overalls and soft shoes. A rope to his bosun's harness is held by an assistant while he works himself underneath the apex of the derrick, so that he can hitch himself to the main line over the pulley. He is then attached to both main and safety lines and, when secure, he releases the rope held by the assistant. In March 1978 a pulley block broke, causing Garry Russell to drop a heart-beat, until he pulled up a few feet down the cliff when the rope to which he was tied became taut again.

Aerial view of Beachy Head looking west, from Whitbread Hollow (near right) to beyond Seaford Head in the distance {Eastbourne Tourism & Leisure}

A Dew Pond near the entrance to Black Robin Farm {N Taylor}

From near the summit the Beachy Head cliffs dwarf the lighthouse

The lighthouse against the background of the Beachy Head cliffs {D Ellwood}

From Belle Tout looking east, showing how close the road runs to the cliff edge.
The lighthouse is to the right and the hotel is just visible on the left skyline

Belle Tout ex-lighthouse in 1997, from the west. Restored, but near the cliff edge

Visitors sitting on the edge of the cliff watching a coastguard rescue exercise

The Seven Sisters, looking east from Seaford Head, with Birling Gap beyond. In the foreground are the Cuckmere Haven coastguard cottages

A flexible ladder (a "Scotsman"), a few metres in length, with widely spaced metre-long wooden rungs is unrolled over the edge of the cliff to make it easier to climb up and over the edge. It also reduces the falls of chalk. As Garry Russell says, 'The most difficult part is getting the rescuer and his burden back over the angle of the edge.'

The capstan pays out the main line (any safety line being simultaneously let out manually) and the rescuer is lowered out over the cliff, either walking down the cliff face or touching with his toes every few metres in abseiling fashion. Along with the lightweight stretcher he can be lowered or raised in a few minutes.

If the situation requires a two-man cliff team, the second man descends on the main line with the safety line left down for the first man. After they have strapped the victim in the stretcher, one rescuer goes up on the main line guiding the stretcher and load, while the second man comes up later.

The auxiliary helpers, apart from setting up the derrick, also pay out the ropes, run the winch motor and give directions to the rescueman.

On occasions, when the victim needs urgent help and speed is essential, the cliff rescueman does not wait for all his assistants to reach the scene before lowering himself down. When a woman fell 20m, on 4 March 1988, auxiliary coastguard Bob Jewson had himself lowered, as soon as he reached the scene, by means of a rope attached to a JCB digger and payed out by police officers. He stayed with the victim, who survived the fall, until fellow coastguard Chris "Twinkletoes" Turner could reach her with a stretcher.

At certain places such as Birling Gap where the cliffs are more regular and only some 30m high, the rescue team may use a slightly different technique. The line is played out over a wooden roller attached to an angle piece which fits snugly on the cliff edge. This simple arrangement facilitates the smooth running of the rope without chaffing, but it does mean that the rescueman has to climb over the roller on the way down and back.

The shortest time for a rescue is about half-an-hour. A precise timetable is available for the recovery of a 54-year-old female in July 1975 from the base of 137m high cliffs.

message received by coastguards	1803h
coastguard crew reached the position ...	1836h
Garry Russell descended cliff	1902h
body located	1912h
returned to the top with the body	1937h

If the person is on a ledge recovery can be impressively speedy. In 1973 a 51-year-old was seen to fall at 2030h and was recovered from a ledge 45m down at 2120h. In 1971 a 38-year-old male was seen to push off at 1150h and was recovered from 45m down at 1245h. The same year a 44-year-old woman jumped at 1230h and was recovered from 60m down at 1335h. On the other hand, also in 1971 and only 75m along the cliff from where the woman jumped, the recovery of the body of a 32-year-old male from a mere 35m down was so difficult that it had to be left until the next day. In January 1982 a 44-year-old woman wasn't found until the next day, and the recovery took coastguard, Ivor Pollard, over two hours.

Rescues have taken over six hours at a time, and have extended over two days. The coastguards are most hampered by instability of the cliff or inclement weather. In the November 1974 recovery of a 52-year-old man, Garry Russell descended in conditions of low cloud, poor visibility and such a gusty wind that Constable DA Jeavons, one of his assistants on the Downs, was blown to the ground. The operation started at 1430h, the body (only 100m down) was not found until 1540h and it took until 1635h to bring it to the cliff top.

Cliff rescueman about to descend, using the lightweight derrick

In 1975 another rescue under difficult weather conditions took four hours. During the descent Garry Russell describes looking about him when all he could see were his ropes disappearing up into thick cloud. For a recovery on 17 May 1979, when the coroner's officer, Mick Davey, said a wind of Beaufort force 6 was blowing, Garry Russell was congratulated by Edward Grace, the deputy coroner.

Even under ideal conditions it is not always possible to locate the victim quickly. During one incident, when a member of the public reported seeing a body at the base of the cliffs, the coastguard was lowered five times without success and finally recovered the body the next day - half a mile from the earlier search area. When another passer-by discovered a 60-year-old at the cliff base in December 1995, it meant a long and difficult rescue operation because of the site.

For the recovery of a 53-year-old man in August 1987, just east of Devil's Chimney, coastguard Bob Cooley required unusual assistance in the form of a 14lb-sledgehammer to break rocks between which the body was jammed.[2]

Recoveries are not usually pursued at night unless there is a chance of saving life. On 1 August 1987, a visitor, Welsh quarry worker Peter Foot, found a torch near the edge and on hearing faint cries for help, clambered down some 60m to reach a 24-year-old Poole man who had slid on to a ledge. Both were winched to safety in a three-hour rescue under searchlights.[3]

Police bravery

Police Constable Richard Harris has been closely concerned with more than one rescue. On a freezing, blustery February day in 1981 a call was received that a man had been seen sitting on the cliffs. When PC Harris and Garry Russell arrived they espied a man's blue anorak seven metres down the cliff face on a ledge overhanging a vertical 50m drop to the beach. PC Harris talked to the man while the coastguard went for his rescue harness. At that moment the man started to slip and the policeman decided that he must act immediately, 'I slid down and fortunately my motor cycle uniform, with the heavy boots, was a great help.'

Fearing that the man would take both of them over, PC Harris struggled to keep hold of him, in the face of gale force winds and with the chalk crumbling beneath his feet. The policeman then realised that the man was a glue sniffer and in his confused state he was impeding the rescue efforts. PC Harris resolved to push the man up the face of the cliff, which he managed by brute strength until he received assistance at the cliff top.

At a special ceremony at Lewes on 20 May 1982 he was presented with the Queen's Commendation for Bravery and the decoration of two silver oak leaves from Lord Abergavenny, Lord Lieutenant for East Sussex.[4] PC Harris said, 'I don't think it was any different from what any other police officer would have done. At the time my only thought was that if I didn't go down to him he would have gone over.' He described his job in the Police as "fantastic" even if at times it did bring him into contact with the sadder results of Beachy Head incidents. 'It was a great feeling to be able to bring someone back alive this time.'

In January 1985 it was announced that the same PC Richard Harris, now 39, was to receive a Royal Humane Society bravery award for saving another potential victim. The previous June a man had dialled 999 and warned police of his intention to end his life. PC Harris reached Beachy Head to see the caller run towards the edge, vault a fence, and sit, crying, with his legs dangling over a 120m drop of notoriously brittle chalk. The constable, assisted by PCs Robin Hodgkinson and Rod Smith, spoke to the man and managed to calm him a little. An hour of talk passed before PC Harris - saying that he could not hear the man's conversation clearly - persuaded him to move away from the edge so that the policemen could pull him to safety.[5]

All three constables received certificates for their bravery from the Mayor of Eastbourne, Councillor Leslie Mason, in April 1985.

The cliffs at Falling Sands erode rapidly and leave unstable chalk balanced over the head of any rescuer. When a 37-year-old woman was recovered in October 1989, Mr Garry Russell said it was one of the most dangerous retrievals ever and that demolition by explosives of the cliff face was needed to render it safe. 'The rock face is eroding leaving tons of unstable chalk balanced precariously over the head of any coastguard.'

Rescues up and down the years

In spite of these dangers, cliff rescues from Beachy Head have been known for centuries. There was the September 1856 rescue of a fossil hunter who climbed half way up and was trapped overnight. He clung to a grassy ledge until first light when he attracted the attention of some fishermen. The coastguards

Coastguard Bob Jewson going down the cliff face, with stretcher

were called and they lowered a rope to enable him to clamber up the remaining 200 feet.

Over the years there have been many stirring tales of courage and heroic rescues. In October 1906 a yacht, the *Gwalia,* broke her cable in a high wind and drifted ashore under Beachy Head.[6] The two men on board managed to scramble to the beach whereupon the yacht slid away. They decided to ascend the cliff until they soon found themselves trapped, unable to continue the ascent or to descend.

Chief Officer Hogben and Coastguard Bridgeman went over the cliff, each at the end of a rope in a wind so strong that they were blown backwards and forwards like pendulums. After what seemed an eternity the rescuers arrived on a ledge 30m above the one on which the yachtsmen were huddled. George Hogben untied his rope and lowered his companion who brought the yachtsmen up to the ledge and the four - rescued and rescuers - were eventually hauled to the cliff top.

A girl was discovered lying on a ledge 120m down the cliff at Coney Bottom, in August 1908. Chief Officer Hogben was lowered to the spot, but the girl screamed when he reached her and as soon as he touched her she fainted. Mr Hogben was only able to hang on to her with great difficulty, but eventually he managed to fasten a rope around her limp body and taking her in his arms he signalled to be hauled up. He reached the top of the cliff with his burden to the cheers of the spectators who had gathered there.

Chief Officer Hartfield had a narrow escape when retrieving the body of a woman in October 1925. He descended to within seven metres of the body but, having untied his rope ready to attach it to the body, he slipped in crossing a ledge and fell some distance, only managing to save himself by clutching at a piece of rock which fortunately held firm.

Garry Russell makes a successful return to the cliff top with an injured victim

In March 1961, Cecil Dann and George Worsell received the Queen's Commendation for brave conduct. This followed a most gallant rescue, on 9 September 1960, when a man was trapped on the cliff face at Falling Sands after trying to retrieve his tent which had blown over.

The police equipment at Beachy Head was not suitable for this rescue and Ivan Worsell, the officer-in-charge (and brother of George) arrived at the cliff top with rope ladders. Three 120-foot lengths of rope ladder were lowered and George Worsell and Cecil Dann began their descent, made difficult by the ladders becoming fouled and twisted by the irregular cliff. The ladders were too short to reach the stranded man so a rope hawser was added, down which the two rescuers were able to reach their goal after three hours.

It took another one and a half hours to haul the three men to the top, over crumbling and falling chalk. The rescued man, an 18-year-old from Addiscombe, was uninjured apart from shock and exposure.[7]

Cecil Arthur Dann was involved in organising another rescue, this time of three fishermen trapped at the base of cliffs near Birling Gap, in November 1971. For this he was awarded a Royal Humane Society testimonial on parchment.

The Worsell brothers concerned in the 1960 rescue (brother Charles was another coastguard) are typical of the local coastguard families with a tradition of facing the perils of the sea. Their father was in the service in the days when the coastguards and customs men were controlled by the Admiralty and carried a cutlass issued for protection against smugglers. George Worsell could remember when horses were used to transport rocket flares to the Coastguard Station. In turn his son, Richard, became an auxiliary at Birling Gap.

Downs Ranger, Police Constable Harry Ward, was awarded the BEM in the 1964 New Year Honours List. He designed a special light alloy stretcher for use on the cliffs and was involved in many hazardous rescues, one in particular in August 1955, when he was lowered 120m in heavy rain in an attempt to save the life of a 66-year-old woman. That same year he had been presented with an RSPCA certificate for rescuing a dog trapped in a fissure 30m from the top. Downs Ranger, PC Jack Williams, rescued a 15-year-old boy from about 100m down in 1967.

Rescues have continued and now include not only climbers, ramblers and would-be suicides, but also hang-glider pilots, model aeroplane enthusiasts, adventurous foreign students, and sheep - to say nothing of the dogs.

Holidaymakers, unfamiliar with the local conditions, not infrequently find themselves stranded - physically - on the cliffs. In July 1974 a 19-year-old trainee accountant on vacation from Peterborough discovered a path near the cliff edge about 150m east of the lighthouse, where the cliffs are about 160m high. Some ten metres down the path he slipped. He recovered himself but, 'the soft chalk kept crumbling in my hands and my feet kept slipping. I was only wearing plimsolls. Eventually I decided it would be better if I just stayed on a ledge and waited for my friend to come back. I was really quite scared by this time.'

After he had been marooned on the ledge for half an hour he was seen by a sharp-sighted passenger on one of the pleasure boats which ply on trips around the lighthouse. The captain of the boat contacted the police who notified the coastguards and it took Garry Russell, Barry Lee and Harry Morley with their experience and equipment a mere matter of minutes to make the rescue, leaving the survivor with only a few bruises to show for his escapade.[8]

There was a similar story on 5 April 1980, which developed into a midnight drama when a 17-year-old youth from Croydon, on a touring holiday with his parents, stopped for the evening at Beachy Head. He wanted to get down to the beach and decided to climb down a 100m cliff near Falling Sands.

At 2215h one of the Beachy Head lighthousemen heard someone calling from the cliffs and alerted the Coastguard Service. Garry Russell climbed down to find the youth perched on a ledge less than a metre long and barely 30cm in depth. The boy was so cold it was reasoned he would not be able to cooperate with the rescue team in getting him to the top of the cliff so Garry sat with him while a helicopter from RAF Manston, Kent was called in. The helicopter was over the spot at 21 minutes past midnight and the rescue completed by 41 minutes past. The boy, taken to the local District General Hospital, was detained suffering from exposure, but he recovered sufficiently to be released later that day.[9]

A fear of being cut off by the tide is often given as a reason by visitors for climbing the cliffs. Garry Russell says, 'Ideally backtrack, if you can't then aim for

Night rescue 1 August 1987, helper Peter Foot being brought back to the cliff top

high ground above high water, such as a rock fall, and wait for the tide to ebb'.

Three German students (a 15-year-old and two 16-year-olds from Berlin) were cut off by the tide on the afternoon of 4 April 1980 and required rescue by helicopter after attempting to climb a 150m high cliff at Gun Gardens. One of them said, 'We were walking along the beach and decided to rest for a while. We forgot the time and about an hour later discovered we had been cut off by the tide. There was no way we could get back along the beach so we started to climb up the cliff. After we got part of the way up my two friends slipped and one was hurt. It was then we got scared and began shouting for help.'

The three were located after their shouts for help were heard coming from the cliffs. The two uninjured students were airlifted out of danger from the rocky beach under Gun Gardens while a 16-year-old, who was slightly injured, was brought up in a two-hour rescue led by Garry Russell. After a check-up at a local hospital he was discharged.

Three months later on the 20 July, two Spanish students, aged 16 and 17, had to be rescued from the cliff after trying to climb down. They were noticed, stuck 30m from the bottom of 100m cliffs at Falling Sands, by a party of canoeists paddling from Cuckmere Haven to Eastbourne. The canoeists went to the lighthouse, raised the alarm and their leader went back to the shore below the students to mark the place for the rescuers. Garry Russell was lowered down the cliff and assisted the students to safety. They were also taken to an Eastbourne hospital and released without requiring treatment.

The Downs and Beachy Head are popular for so many sporting activities that inevitably some work is produced for the rescue teams.

On 8 October 1978 a 38-year-old Tunbridge Wells man had been flying a radio controlled model glider plane most of the day with his young son. At 1800h it fell over the cliff opposite the hotel and on to a ledge. The father climbed down about 30m, but could not reach the plane and then found he could not get back to the cliff top either. He was trapped for the next hour whilst his son alerted the police and Garry Russell came to the rescue aided, on this occasion, by auxiliary coastguard Barry Lee. And what happened to the model plane? In spite of all retrieval attempts it fell off the ledge and was lost on the rocks below.[10]

Hang gliders also use Beachy Head cliffs, although the local councillors wax and wane in their desire to encourage or ban the activity. Such a sport is bound to occasion employment for the local rescue services.

In the late 1970s there would be perhaps 25 hang gliders at Beachy Head on a suitable day and for one Newport man his first day there was almost his last. He took off on April Fool's Day, 1978 at 1900h, from near the lighthouse in his Waspair Gryphon glider. An eye witness said, 'He took off from the top of the cliffs, but soon began to lose height. He tried to land, lost more height and had to descend to the beach. He is an experienced flier and he made a controlled landing on a stretch of shingle.' The pilot was unhurt, but he was trapped by the tide and needed Garry Russell to be winched down to help both him and glider, worth about £600, up the cliff face. With no hitches except a few scratches on the glider, the whole recovery took just 45 minutes.

Later the same month on St George's Day, a French hang glider pilot on a weekend trip to England was not so fortunate. The 29-year-old Frenchman borrowed a glider from Miles Haneley, a Sussex glider designer, and launched himself off well enough, and was just about to touch down again when turbulence, from the air currents which whip across the cliffs, dragged him sideways off the edge. Police Constable Tom Day, who was called to the incident said, 'He tried to regain control as he dropped downwards. He managed to do this at the last moment, but failed to make a proper landing.' The pilot broke an arm and a leg after plunging the 100m or so to the rocky shore at Falling Sands and was taken off to safety by Eastbourne's inshore rescue boat. He was admitted to hospital where next day he was described as "comfortable". The designer who had lent his glider was also unfortunate in that it was badly damaged.[11]

The modern rescue service enlists all available assistance, from medical needs to inshore rescue boats, helicopters and lifeboats.

As mentioned in the Lifeboat section (Chapter 2), lifeboats are rarely needed for the purposes of cliff rescue, although the Eastbourne or Newhaven lifeboats often stand off ready to give assistance. Even when, in June 1987, a 27-year-old man fell on to the beach near Cow Gap, the sea was too choppy to use the inshore rescue lifeboat. PC Paul Budgen with ambulancemen abseiled down to him, coastguards Bob Cooley, Pete Lewis attended, and a standard helicopter rescue was mounted.

When injury has been sustained, where access is difficult, or when lengthy transport of the victim is involved, helicopter transfer is used. It has been shown to reduce mortality and morbidity, although the cost is substantial.

Latterly, helicopters have been used as the most suitable method of rescue even if the trapped person is uninjured. An adventurous 23-year-old from Essex found himself stuck on a ledge when climbing down a cliff on 27 May 1985. He attracted the attention of the crew of a passing fishing boat, who alerted the emergency services and the uninjured man was winched to safety by helicopter.

The medical and allied professions are always ready to assist in rescues whenever urgent medical attention is necessary for those trapped on the cliffs. When in July 1979 a woman was found severely injured on a ledge 55m down a 130m cliff, Garry Russell was first to attend to her and because a doctor was not immediately available, a St John Ambulance Brigade member, 24-year-old Graham Andrews, volunteered to climb down to the casualty and give first aid. Dr NR Sargant, who reached the patient shortly afterwards, said he was impressed by the ambulance man's calm behaviour and he deserved the highest praise. In the spring of the following year at a ceremony attended by Eastbourne's Mayor and Mayoress, Mr and Mrs Joseph Angelman, Divisional Officer Andrews was awarded the silver bar and meritorious service certificate by the County Commissioner Mr Kenneth Bolton.[12]

The Police Surgeons help when needed. Dr DG Churcher, the Police Surgeon from before the 1939-45 war, must have been involved in over a hundred Beachy Head cases. When he retired in 1975 he was succeeded by Dr Robert Rew, with Dr DAH Ashforth as deputy. In 1991 Dr Rew handed over to Dr Jozef Ludwig.

In 1976 when an injured victim was found on the cliffs, Dr Rew was lowered to her for his own first experience of cliff rescue work. He was to attend on three occasions over the next four years.

Dr Rew said that, while he was saddened by the human tragedies which unfolded, he found a quiet enjoyment in the rescue experience. 'I think it's whether you have a head for heights or not. I did quite a bit of climbing, especially as a student. The main difficulty is the cold and the wind. I'm sure it is easier now than in the days of rope ladders, or being lowered down hanging on to the end of a rope. I don't think that Nick Sargant, one of my partners, enjoyed the time he had to go over on an occasion when I was on leave, but I find it's a change from a routine surgery. To compensate my partners who may have to do extra surgery work for me, I pay 25% of my Police Surgeon earnings into the practice.'

Asked whether he felt safe when on the cliff face, Dr Rew replied 'I did not feel insecure. I was firmly harnessed with a thick rope to a winch on a Land Rover above. I wasn't likely to pull that over.'

Helicopter rescue at Beachy Head {Beckett Newspapers}

After the 1978 rescue of a woman who survived a 90m fall, Eastbourne's deputy police commander, Chief Inspector Peter Sharpe, said of Dr Rew, who had agreed to descend the cliff without hesitation, 'No praise is too high for that man - it was an extremely courageous effort.'

No veterinary surgeons have been lowered down the cliffs as yet, but rescues and recoveries are often needed for dogs.

On 27 January 1980 a family from Forest Row was out for a walk on the Downs with their Dalmatian when it ran to the cliff edge and fell over. It landed on a ledge, but in struggling up, missed its footing and fell hundreds of feet to the beach. Garry Russell was lowered to recover the body.[13]

There was a happier result when a Jack Russell fell at the Whitbread Hollow cliffs on Thursday afternoon, 7 September 1978. Barry Lee climbed down 25m and with the aid of a harness returned the dog safely to its owners.

In January 1989 a two-year-old black Spaniel, *Khara,* not only escaped with just a few bruises after falling to the beach at Whitbread Hollow, but was the first pet to be rescued by helicopter. As a police spokesman said, 'People often hail down police cars, but this is the first time anyone has flagged down our new police helicopter out on a routine exercise.'

According to the *Eastbourne Herald* of 7 August 1982, a slight variation in animal rescues happened when *Penny*, a greyhound, got herself onto a ledge during a beach walk with her Eastbourne family and then concluded that she couldn't get off again. Her owner managed to climb up to her, but slipped and had to let go, so he telephoned the coastguards and within minutes Garry Russell was lowering himself towards *Penny*. Being a shy female, she would have nothing to do with this stranger and finally it was necessary for her owner to be lowered down to help Garry. She suffered the embarrassment of being hauled up in a net, although otherwise no worse for her experience.

Avoidance is better than cure even for cliff rescues and the police are often involved in preventative measures, with the general public playing their part as well. When a 50-year-old woman from Cheam, Surrey, was stuck on a ledge about four metres down the cliff face on 9 August 1964, she was pulled back to the top by Mrs C Hollingsdale, who lived nearby.

In January 1983 a Bedfordshire woman was saved by the timely counselling of Mrs Kate Guy of Eastbourne who, when walking on the Downs, saw the woman crying bitterly on the nearby cliffs and asked if she could be of some help. At first the woman refused to move from her precarious perch, but gradually she was enticed into Mrs Guy's car and then to her home where the woman's husband in Dunstable was called to take his wife home.[14]

Every year the police stop likely falls by the thoroughness of their investigations and a sympathetic approach. At 1930h on 24 January 1978 a car was found abandoned on a grass verge near the cliff top. A computer check of the registration number revealed that the vehicle was owned by a 24-year-old woman from Guildford known to have suicidal tendencies. Further information was radioed to the cliff top that a man from Croydon was missing. Within 40 minutes the woman was found walking along a path near Whitbread Hollow and shortly afterwards the man was seen in a car park. Both were taken to hospital.

More smart work by Eastbourne police enabled them to return a 63-year-old Coventry man to his family after he had been discovered in an upset state at Beachy Head in the early hours of Boxing Day 1982.

A mammoth Giro cheque fraud ended at Beachy Head. The culprit, a 26-year-old Epsom man, who had been a patient at Broadmoor, found work after his release and opened a Giro account with £23. He then went on a spending spree, having been provided with no less than five cheque books. He attempted suicide with tablets, which he followed by an attempt at Beachy Head when he tried to drive a car over. By good fortune the police had been alerted and by ramming his car they saved his life. In February 1983 he was the subject of a three-year probation order on charges of obtaining property by deception.[15]

Saturday, 31 July 1976, saw the coastguards prepare for a rescue, but stand aside for an attempt by policemen to persuade a 16-year-old youth to move to safety. A 999 emergency call had alerted the coastguards to a youth who appeared to be about to jump. He was discovered sitting on an outcrop about 30m down the cliff, at a point half way between the, then, Police Box and lighthouse. The police managed to convince the youth that he should climb back up the cliff. He was taken to the police station before being released into the care of his parents with, thankfully, no further involvement from the coastguards required that day.[16]

There was a similar episode on 8 February 1972. A young man perched himself on a ledge two metres from the cliff top, about 250m east of the lighthouse at a point called the Pulpit. Speaking to a policeman, he said that no one wanted him and he was going to throw himself off. Fortunately, after 30 minutes' conversation he agreed to be hauled to safety.

There have been many occasions at Beachy Head when the police have saved a life by their timely action. In the summer of 1978 Police Constable Brian Richardson dashed to the cliff top after receiving information that a woman had gone to Beachy Head to commit suicide. He saw the woman and approached her slowly, but as he neared her she stepped off the edge. At that moment PC Richardson grabbed at her and held on to her anorak, even though her weight started to drag him over with her. Finally, with the help of a holidaymaker he was able to pull her to safety. The 38-year-old policeman was awarded the Queen's Commendation for Brave Conduct for his part in the rescue.[17] In 1981 PC Richardson took over as the Downs Ranger.

Another rescue was on Sunday, 8 May 1983, when the police received a call saying that a man was standing on the edge of the cliffs to the east of Devil's Chimney. Police officers were able to drag the 33-year-old Gravesend man away. He had taken a drug overdose and was admitted to hospital.

A Woman Police Constable was involved in preventing a Beachy Head death plunge in January 1985 when she sat on the cliff edge for 30 minutes talking to a distressed woman until her colleagues were able to reach the woman and pull her to safety. In the October WPC Julie Bettis, Sergeant Andy Humphreys and PC Dave Mallon received Royal Humane Society awards for their brave work.[18]

The rescues continue for in June 1990 PC Ivan Huff saved a 16-year-old girl by grabbing her pony tail as she leapt over. He pulled her back with the help of PC Mark Tucker.[19] Almost exactly three years later, a 29-year-old male was seen sitting on the edge. After being roped, PC John Devlin sat with him on the edge, with Inspector Martin Stevens, also roped, sitting on the other side, and PC Trevor Perks and PC Steven Vodrey were nearby. The Inspector offered him a cigarette and as he went to light it they all pulled him back. In 1994 all were given Bravery Awards from the Royal Humane Society.[20] In 1995 Inspector Malcolm Richards and PC Nick Flude rescued a man who fell at Holywell.

Hoaxes

Not all efforts have such a worthy conclusion. On 18 September 1978 the police received a telephone call that a woman had gone to Beachy Head threatening to kill herself. When two officers went to the cliff top they saw a 23-year-old Eastbourne woman staggering about in a drunken state and waving a knife at them. A week later she was fined a total of £50 for being drunk and disorderly and having with her in a public place an offensive weapon.

Whatever the method of rescue and whoever is rescued, such work is dangerous and it is vital that no undue risks are taken. It is a truism, however, that where human tragedy exists, whether it be bomb warnings or fire alerts, there will be the false alarm. This may follow a misunderstanding, sometimes there is malicious intent, and not uncommonly it is a so-called joke by bored youngsters or disturbed individuals. Beachy Head has had its share.

Needless "rescues" are sometimes made with the best of intentions; for instance, on 5 October 1964 PC Harry Ward was lowered 30m (100 ft) down to a ledge only to discover the supposed "body" to be a black raincoat lost on the cliff. Unfortunately, there are examples of hoaxes - varying from the placing of a pile of clothes on the top of the cliff, as on 17 November 1937, to spurious telephone calls - which have produced extra work and unnecessary danger.

At 2100h on Thursday, 28 June 1979 a woman telephoned the coastguard and said that a boy aged 14 had fallen over.[21] The circumstances were especially poignant for only in the May a 14-year-old Dutch boy had accidentally fallen to his death and the call was traced to the public telephone box on the Downs near Beachy Head, nevertheless the police were unable to find the caller. Garry Russell called out his rescue team and made a thorough search of the area, including the use of a police tracker dog, and when daylight came an RAF helicopter checked the cliffs - all without result.

On 25 March 1980 there was a call direct to the coastguard, again in the evening about 2130h. A female voice said she was telephoning from the call box at Beachy Head and added, 'I am going to jump' as she slammed the receiver down. Coastguards and police searched the cliffs that night and continued the next day without finding any sign of the woman.[22]

A deceptive "John Stonehouse or Reggie Perrin" type of hoax was perpetrated at Beachy Head in July 1989 when an abandoned car was found, with a bottle of pills, a bottle of vodka and two lengthy suicide notes inside. The owner, a 26-year-old High Wycombe father of six, turned up at his home three months later.

Cars, or their misuse, provide further work. They have been backed up to the cliff edge (perhaps to tip out an old piano or bedstead) and then carefully driven away along the same tracks. Such actions, giving the impression that a van has driven over, produce consternation the next morning. It is also not uncommon for "joy riders" cars to be pushed over. All these incidents require police investigation.

On 12 January 1959 a *Vauxhall Velox* fell 150m near the lighthouse; the number plates had been removed and there was no sign of a driver. The next year, on St Valentine's Day a black *Wolseley* went over 200m east of the lighthouse - it had been stolen in Finchley. On 28 April 1963 a green *Hillman Husky* was found at the foot of the cliffs below Belle Tout with no one in or around the car.

Until the last decade the major supplier of distorted boxes rusting away at the base of Beachy Head had been the British motor industry. Over the last few years, in line with trends in car ownership, overseas makes have succeeded in penetrating this very open market.

The result of a Renault travelling at 500 feet in five seconds

A yellow *Lada* was seen on the beach between Belle Tout and Birling Gap on 19 June 1980. The coastguards searched for two hours and found several articles of clothing, but no body and, as the number plates had been removed, the conclusion was that the car had been abandoned.[23] In September 1983 a green T-registered *Renault* was seen by the police lying at the foot of a sheer 135m drop at Devil's Chimney. A routine search of the nearby cliff was instituted, and auxiliary coastguards Bob Jewson and Robin Jefford lowered, but without result.

In recent years earth banks have been raised near the roadside to hamper cliff access by cars and thus reduce the number of accidents.

This is perhaps the moment for a special mention of Garry Russell who retired in 1995. He would be the first to acknowledge that he is a representative of the local coastguard service and only one of the many officers and volunteers who man the watches and are ready for duty at any time.

Garry David Russell saw service in the Royal Navy. He decided to join the Coastguard Service and came to Eastbourne in 1967, becoming station officer-in-charge in 1973. He is married with three children, Elaine, Audrey and David.[24]

As officer-in-charge he initiated and coordinated search and rescue operations at sea and arranged rescues with sea-to-shore equipment when ships were in trouble not too far from the shore. Cliff rescues were one of his main jobs and he has been lowered down the cliff face in all conditions of hail and gale as part of his responsibilities. Even with ropes that have a four-and-a-half-ton breaking strain the dangers of cliff work are immense.

In the 20 years from October 1973 Mr Russell saved 21 persons, recovered over 100 bodies, rescued 14 dogs and only twice gave up in the middle of a recovery because of bad weather. He made his last descent on 3 October 1993.

Garry thinks that he has done more cliff work than anyone else in the country. 'I used to mark incidents on the map - now there's not enough space. The summer is the peak time. If it's any consolation, most wanted to be there.'

He went on, 'One of these days there could be a serious chalk fall while the coastguards are carrying out a recovery operation. The crowds who clamour to watch a Beachy Head recovery put themselves at risk as well as the coastguards.' His wife, Rosemary, tried not to worry when he was involved in a dangerous mission, 'I knew,' she said, 'he would not take unnecessary risks ... It's his life and I'm so proud of him sometimes I could cry.'

The award of a British Empire Medal in the 1980 New Year Honours List was greeted with general acclaim and satisfaction. The East Sussex coroner at the time, Mr John Dodd, publicly congratulated him, praising his work and saying that the honour was 'thoroughly well deserved.'

Garry Russell pays the highest tribute to the local coastguard auxiliaries. 'All of them rally round as soon as we send out a call, whatever the weather they do a super job - in wind, hail and rain and there is never a murmur of complaint from any of them. They come from all walks of life and they are the best comrades you could wish for, among us there is a splendid esprit de corps.'

6   CLIMBING

Near a point opposite the lighthouse is an outcrop of chalk, a column standing out towards the sea, known as the Devil's Chimney.

In the days before British climbers discovered the attractions of the Alps, this spot at Beachy Head was a popular climbing place. On the stretch from Holywell to Falling Sands there are many easy routes for a climber of poor agility to scramble up from the shore, but from near the lighthouse to Birling Gap the heights present no easy access, and just east of the present lighthouse was the climbing area in Victorian times.

In the last century there were three easily distinguishable pinnacles of chalk, named from east to west - "Split Block", "Etheldreda's Pinnacle" and "Devil's Chimney". They were the relics of seven or more chalk pillars standing out from the cliff (in the fashion of the Needles at the Isle of Wight) and known locally as the Charleys or, even more improbably, the Charleses; as MA Lower writes, "When the Charleses wear a cap the clouds weep".

Around 1900 it was said the Devil's Chimney was the second "Charles", and the third was destroyed in the making of the new lighthouse in 1902. All along here the relatively soft rock is continuously eroded: one outcrop being destroyed and another separating from the main cliff and the names being perpetuated. They are always about to disappear; in 1853 Madock said the last had disappeared, while Bourdillon said at least three had survived to 1884. One Devil's Chimney is said to have subsided into the sea in the 1950s leaving only Etheldreda's Pinnacle, which everyone calls the Devil's Chimney.

In 1868/69 Lord Hobhouse and Mr WE Forster MP independently climbed Beachy Head, and in the second half of the 19th century most of the famed climbers of the time - AF Mummery, FW Bourdillon, Dr TG Longstaff and the Revd Walter Weston - learned to take no liberties with this majestic head and its flowing white beard. It was said to be dazzling in its whiteness in sunshine and even more dangerous in mist or snow. Climbing there became such an attraction that WP Haskett Smith wrote, "... a very fine bold chalk cliff, the first ascent of which is made about once every two years if we may believe all that we see in the papers."[1] Walter Parry Haskett Smith first popularised rock climbing when he scaled Nape's Needle, a 75-foot granite pillar on Great Gable, on 28 June 1886.[2]

Don't Climb Beachy Head

At this juncture it is important to discourage climbing at Beachy Head. It must be stressed that chalk cliffs are not made for safe climbing, they provide no firm holds and foolhardy attempts to climb, or descend, only too often end in disaster. In 1850 the Revd H James, Vicar of Willingdon, on a picnic at Beachy Head attempted to descend to the shore and fell to his death,[3] and in 1863 a taxidermist looking for birds and eggs on the cliff face, "in spite of warnings," slipped and was killed.

Fatalities while climbing are not common because most people are aware of the dangers and climb elsewhere. If they are foolish enough to try, and become stranded, these days they can be rescued from a precarious perch, thanks to the coastguards and helicopters. During the years 1965-89 of 250 deaths on the cliffs only two were from climbing accidents, both young men from London and both possibly under the influence of alcohol or drugs.

Charles Pilkington wrote in the Badminton Library volume on Mountaineering, "...the white cliffs of old England have proved themselves too much for many of her sons. Chalk is a very troublesome material to climb; it is loose, breaks away, and if wet...forms a sticky paste which, lodging between the boot nails, renders them of little use. Doubtless many of those who get into difficulties are only shod for a walk on the promenade or pier, but chalk cliffs must not be treated carelessly even by the well equipped".

So any writer associating chalk and climbing must emphasise that there is no wish to tempt the novice.[4] Chalk climbing and danger are inseparable because there is no sound rock or safeguard for careful belaying. In H Somerset Bullock's words, "There is a certain prejudice against fine grained white non-crystalline, soft limestone,"[5] and Edward Whymper (1840-1911, the first to scale the Matterhorn) relates in his book *Scrambles Amongst the Alps* how he and his schoolboy brother scaled the cliffs at Beachy Head, near Devil's Chimney, "Since then we have often been in danger of different kinds, but never have we more nearly broken our necks than upon that occasion."

About the 1860s, another Alpine climber, John Stogden, was glissading and step-cutting, to which the chalk lends itself. It is soft enough to enable steps to be cut, and steep enough to require them; its disadvantages are the friable nature of the holds. These did not deter the early Alpinists who practised on the cliffs and by the end of the 19th century many routes had been recorded on Beachy Head. Rock climbing was developing fast, however, and as chalk could not fulfil the requirements of the sport, by the turn of the century climbing had ceased at Beachy Head. There are many accounts of those climbing days now passed.

The finest climb at Beachy Head was said to be the ascent of Devil's Chimney, from its base to a gap between it and the top of the cliff. Aleister Crowley (later of strange and unsavoury reputation) and his companion Gregor Grant climbed it in 1894 the other way round from the gap.

Aleister Crowley, whose biography was entitled *The Great Beast,* had many interests especially chess and mountaineering. As an example of his style, during the First World War Crowley wrote that his aunt's suburb near Croydon had been bombed, adding, "Unfortunately her house was not hit. Count Zeppelin is respectfully requested to try again. The exact address is *Eton Lodge,* Outram Road, Addiscombe".

For Crowley, "The fantastic beauty of the cliffs of Beachy Head can never be understood by anyone who has not grappled with them ... they offer rock problems as varied, interesting and picturesque as any cliffs in the world. My association with the Head possesses a Charm which I have never known in any other district of England. My climbs there fulfilled all my ideas of romance, and in addition had the particular delight of complete originality. In other districts I could be no more than *primus inter pares*. On Beachy Head I was the only one - I had invented an entirely new branch of the sport".

Close shave of a climb

With Grant, he climbed the fabulous pinnacle of the Devil's Chimney over two weekends in July 1894, and wrote up an account of his climbs in, of all places, the *Scottish Mountaineering Club Journal.*[6]

"4th July, 1894. We walked along the top of the cliffs till we reached the descent to Pisgah [the main cliff behind the Chimney] on which my friend fixed himself, while I descended the rotten ridge that leads to Jordan [the gap between the Chimney and the main cliff]. Above and beyond rises Few Chimney, perhaps twenty feet high, affording what seemed the only possible access to the Tooth [the inner pinnacle of the Chimney]. By dint of much squirming and the judicious use of such pressure holds as were available, I succeeded in reaching the top of the eastern wall of the chimney, while the summit of the Tooth still towered above me in all its rottenness. Both the north and east faces were coated with loose layers of chalk, which came away with a single touch, but the east had the advantage of being less vertical. After much belabouring of it with my axe I succeeded in reducing it to a condition of comparative stability, and by dint of a few steps and hitching the rope over the top managed to struggle to the summit. The laborious nature of the climb is evidenced by the two hours and more required to overcome a vertical height of only thirty feet. After carefully reconnoitring the Needle [the outer pinnacle], and pronouncing it impossible, I rejoined my friend on Pisgah.

"11th July, 1894. After lunch at the Beachy Head Hotel, we followed the usual route to Pisgah, and then proceeded to the Tooth as before in much less time than on the first ascent. On this Grant fixed himself and I went down the ridge into the Gash [the gap between the inner and outer pinnacles of the Chimney], fixed myself, and began my steps. The chalk is much firmer than on the Tooth, but the north face is, if not undercut, at least vertical, the west overhangs, and the east is about 70* if not more. On the north-east corner, therefore, three steps were cut, going as high as possible to save subsequent work. Five times I tried to cross the Gash, but with no decent handhold it is hardly to be expected that one can pull oneself up to a vertical wall. One chance, however, remained, I scooped out a hole in the east face, inserted my chin and hauled. I had not shaved for a day or two, so was practically enjoying the advantages of Mummery spikes. The extra steadiness proved sufficient, and I came up into a position of the most ticklish balance conceivable, but the next step was easier, and from it I managed to hitch the rope well over. Soon I was able to get my hands on the ridge; my right leg followed, then the rest of my body, and the Needle was conquered. However it is not 'built for two', Grant, much to his disappointment, had to stay on the Tooth, and console himself by hoisting the Union Jack, which we left to wave triumphantly over the scene of our victory."

Crowley, right, and Grant riding the chalk pinnacles of Beachy Head, 1894

Crowley goes on, "Directly I saw [Etheldreda's Pinnacle] I determined to climb it at once. Two chimneys, side by side, and since named Castor and Pollux, presented the most obvious route to the ridge joining the pinnacle with the mass of the cliff. The north one [Castor] looked easy, though it was almost entirely filled with chalk dust of the consistency of fine flour, caked on the top, and having lumps of various sizes in the middle. All this at a touch came down, and the whole weight jammed on my legs, which were well into the chimney. A convulsive series of amoeboid movements enabled me to get out over the debris, when it immediately thundered down, leaving me in a very comfortable gap. I was soon on the ridge. My friend refused to follow, but as he was roped I put on a sudden pressure and he - well - changed his mind. When he reached the ridge I went on for the north face. This has several natural steps. Thence the route lay westwards to the north west corner and then back again, only one step being at all awkward. The summit consists of a big square block, which rocked and swayed under me as I sat down upon it."

Crowley was not always successful. He records having to be rescued by the coastguard after becoming stuck, "Coated in white by the chalk, I had to run the gauntlet of the infidel fashion of Eastbourne and be scorned for a miller or baker".

Bourdillon, writing in 1917 and quoting from a paper given to the Eastbourne Natural History Society in 1893/94 says, "No footholds are worth much. Balance is all important". As the *Sussex County Magazine* put it in 1935, "...you need to know old Beachy and all his shifty ways."[7]

Geoffrey Winthrop Young's book *Mountain Craft,* of 1920, suggests that, "Chalk climbing provides the missing link between rock and ice technique".

WP Haskett Smith thought climbing there had its compensations, "...not for the novice, but it offers rich rewards for the practised climber... Once round the first pinnacle the most magnificent and stupendous of the chalk towers bursts into view. To see it to perfection, give me the dying day when the smouldering glow of sunset fires is behind the tower. Here you can lie and dream between heaven and earth, watching the voyaging of the gulls, the gambols of the little brown rabbits or the summer sleep of young fox cubs. Not a tripper can you see...or imagine such a haven of security and silence."

In 1963 the *Alpine Journal* stated, "The contrasts of the white cliffs against the blue sky above the immensity of the heaving channel far below was... an aesthetic shock to be numbered with Alpine memories".

There were always those who intruded on this idyllic state. Even when Haskett Smith was writing at the turn of the century, a 60-year-old lady with a walking stick and a guide made it to the top of Etheldreda's Pinnacle, and on a Sunday afternoon in November 1898 a soldier, for a bet, attempted to climb the cliffs while carrying a full size bicycle on his back. As was remarked at the time, hardly a safety bicycle! He managed to struggle up some 60m (or 200 feet in Victorian times) until he found his footholds insecure. Happily, one of the bicycle handles became stuck in a crack and he was able to cling on to the machine. A member of the Alpine Club who had been watching from the top climbed down and instructing the soldier to hold on to the bicycle, hauled man and machine to the top with, "one or two pauses for rest."

In March 1929 a young man named Cornish was walking on the beach near the lighthouse when he suddenly realised that the rapidly rising tide would presently cut off his retreat. Without thinking he began to ascend the cliff. "For the first 20 feet or so the cliff was almost perpendicular, but I was able to make progress by means of the many little ledges in the chalk. While I climbed I dared not look down and I realised that the slightest slip would be the end of me. At the height of about 100 feet I found myself clinging to a tuft of grass, with my foot on a little ledge. It was impossible to go down and I thought - 'What am I to do now?' - and although I did carry on I don't know how I did it. The second stage of the climb was not so stiff, but it was a matter of almost 300 feet and several times I thought the next moment was going to be my last. The final stage was also a terrible ordeal of about 200 feet. In one part I got hold of a large projecting flint and was congratulating myself and had just put my weight on it to raise myself, when it came away in my hand. My heart jumped to my mouth, but I was saved by pressing my body against the face of the chalk. When I reached the last six feet I was covered in chalk and perspiration, and wedged in a sort of crevasse, but I managed to extricate myself and reach the top."

More recently in April 1973, Julian Groves, a local 13-year-old, had to be rescued after becoming stuck while bird-nesting on the cliffs.

Two climbing accidents at Beachy Head demonstrate the dangers.

On 20 September 1969 two men decided to make a descent just east of the lighthouse. One said, 'I went first, down a chimney which ended after about 25 feet, when there was a sheer 15 foot to a grassy slope. I began angling down when I heard a scraping sound and saw my companion sliding towards me in a spread-eagled position against the cliff face. I tried to catch him but was unsuccessful'. The witness was guided back to the cliff top by Fire Officer Ody. Later Station Fire Officer Harry Nunn retrieved the body of his 22-year-old companion.

A soldier attempting to climb Beachy Head with a bicycle, 1898

Some ten years later, on 27 July 1979, again two young men decided to climb down the cliff. One of them said, 'My companion's transistor radio fell down onto a ledge and we decided to fetch it. We thought it looked an easy climb from the top and decided to continue climbing. We had got about half-way down where it got very steep. He seemed to know what he was doing, but I was pretty scared'. They realised it was impossible to go any further and started to climb back. 'I started back, but he said he couldn't so I said I would get help. I heard him shout and he slid over a sheer edge.' At the inquest, Mr John Dodd, the coroner, strongly emphasised the dangers of climbing on Beachy Head's chalk cliffs.[8]

Even to-day's seasoned mountain climbers find themselves no match for the unreliable footings of chalk cliffs.

On 11 June 1981 a 23-year-old man, an experienced climber, and a 26-year-old woman companion started on a climb up the cliffs. About 70m from the top they became stuck, close to Devil's Chimney. Police and rescue services who attended brought the rather shaken couple to the top, but they did not require medical attention.[9]

Unusual methods

In the 1930s Frank Illingworth, a bird photographer, made several descents of the cliffs. In 1936 he wrote, "Several people killed this year as a result of falling over Sussex cliffs. I always use two ropes (the rope always looks thinner as you go down and trust your weight to it), wear a tin helmet and bend a piece of corrugated iron over the edge to stop the rope chaffing".

He didn't always take his own advice, for the next year he had himself lowered over the cliff on a rope with no protection to stop it being cut by flints. He was looking for a chough's nest, but didn't find one. Choughs are now unknown, but the sensations described are all too familiar if you look over the edge of the cliff.

A year later Illingworth climbed one of the Seven Sisters with others, aided by ropes and pitons, "Hard, smooth and impossible to climb without pitons."[10]

In recent times several novel ways of descent or ascent have been employed. In 1971, a 26-year-old undergraduate, Michael Taylor, lashed a safety rope to the base of the telegraph pole which was immediately opposite the lighthouse, hurled the free end over the edge and slid down to the beach. He then hauled himself back up the rope and sixteen hours later reached the cliff top again.[11] On 7 April 1980 Police Constable Ivan Huff abseiled down the cliff - after admitting he was scared of heights. He was picked up by an RAF rescue helicopter at the bottom, and his more than 500-foot drop raised over £1000 in sponsorship for the Merchant Navy's Nautical Training Corps.[12] Boxing Day 1988 saw ex-Marine/Sea Scouts, Alan Killick, Mark Allchorn, Andy Murray, Danny Evans, Tony Lumley and Barry George, help digest their Christmas Pud by abseiling down and raising over £500 for the cadets and RNLI.

7 LUCKY ESCAPES

Cardamine Pratensis "Cuckoo Floures"
"Being inwardly taken it is good for
such as have fallen from high places"

Herbal or History of Plants 1633. John Gerard

'Do you know of anyone who fell at Beachy Head and survived?' is a question often asked.

The answer is 'Yes - depending on,' as Professor CEM Joad would say, 'what you mean by a fall.'

Looking at the straight, white face of the Beachy Head cliffs, 400 to 500 feet verticals of undercut chalk with horizontal lines of dark, angular flints, it seems impossible that anyone could survive a fall there. Needless to say, no one has survived a sheer 165m (535 ft) fall down the highest vertical point, but the cliffs vary a great deal with some parts around Cow Gap being not much more than a series of steep, grassy banks interspersed with chalk faces. Even the high, vertical cliffs are often broken by cracks and ledges overgrown with grass and brambles.

The line of cliffs varies not only in height of sheer drop but also in the landing ground. A yielding mattress of turf and bushes requires a great height of fall to ensure fatal injuries.

So, as our "able second-rate philosopher" expected, the unexpected happens.

On 11 August 1972 a 25-year-old Brighton man fell nine metres at Birling Gap when climbing and sustained only cuts and bruises. Again that year on 16 October a London youth attempted to run down part of the cliff after a late night jaunt. He fell 12m and was unconscious when found, but recovered fully. Another Brighton man, aged 27, tumbled more than 15m down the cliff face in March 1979 before his fall was halted by a jutting out ledge. He was seen by one of the lighthouse keepers who alerted the coastguard team. By the time the team arrived the young man was already trying to climb back and he was assisted up by the coastguards who found his only injuries were a few cuts and bruises.[1]

It is thus important to define "A Fall at Beachy Head" - perhaps in more ways than one. In September 1982 a 79-year-old Eltham woman broke her hip in a fall at Beachy Head, and her surgeon, Mr DJ Richards, wondered if she could be included as an example of "Falling at Beachy Head". She had, he explained, 'Slipped on the wet floor of the ladies' lavatory at the top of the cliff'. Again, some years ago one of the local obstetricians, Mr JR Shardlow, enquired whether a patient of his qualified. At the ante natal clinic she had confided to him that she, 'Fell pregnant on the Downs at Beachy Head'.

There are also survivors of falls in which the authentication of the distance fallen is unsure; for example, a boy was said to have fallen 400 feet in 1967 and lived, and a woman 100 feet in 1989. Such falls have not been included, and for the purpose of answering the question "Did anyone fall and survive?" the definition of a "Fall" at Beachy Head will be a proven drop of at least 20 metres (65 feet), and "Survival" implies recovery. Some residual incapacity is accepted, but victims found alive only to die later of their injuries are excluded.

As defined, between 1964 and 1990, 12 persons fell at Beachy Head and survived.

Two escapes were in the summer of 1976. One was the terrifying accident, referred to in Chapter 1, of a 12-year-old Dagenham girl who fell 100 feet down a fissure, the other was a well-documented fall of a 72-year-old London woman.

The fissure down which a 12-year-old girl fell in July 1976

On Monday, 5 July 1976, the 12-year-old was on holiday in Eastbourne with her school. One of a group of 36 children and three teachers on a footpath overlooking the lighthouse, she was walking a few feet from the cliff edge when she fell and disappeared from view. The little girl had plunged to the bottom of a fissure about five metres in length, one metre wide and 30m deep, from where her friends could hear her frantic cries for help.

Police and emergency services were alerted. Auxiliary coastguard Barry Lee was lowered into the fissure to ensure she was properly strapped into a safety harness and she was hauled up within half an hour. The girl's first words were to apologise for being 'a nuisance'. She was released from the local hospital the next day having suffered only bruises and scratches.[2]

She was very lucky, as she had no warning of the danger and if alone, she could have been trapped at the bottom of the deep ravine. The multiple cracks in the cliffs are normally covered by a layer of earth, but there is no easy way of knowing how deep they are until they are extended or eroded and the earth plug falls away. This fissure had widened during the dry, sunny summer of 1976.

In the other escape a 72-year-old was admitted to a local hospital at 1830h on

92

Sunday, 2 May, having fallen some 25m. Her landing, on a narrow ledge, had been cushioned by grass. She was conscious, but suffered bruising of her head with a laceration on the front of her scalp and abrasions. She had fractures of her limbs, spine and ribs.

She was an in-patient at a Norwich psychiatric hospital where she had been until 1000h on the morning of the day she fell.

She said that she sat on the edge of the cliff for some time and had even asked a passer-by to give her a push off. Before he could react she slipped over and the alarm was raised by a sightseer who saw her plunge down the cliffs opposite the Beachy Head Hotel. Coastguards sped to the scene although it was 30 minutes before she was located on the ledge. Garry Russell, coastguard-in-charge, summoned Police Surgeon, Dr Robert Rew, to ensure that she had every chance of recovery and the doctor joined the coastguard on the ledge 15 minutes later. The rescue was watched by nearly 100 people.[3]

Dr Rew said, 'It was remarkable the woman did not suffer more injuries, especially as she was 72. I think her life was saved by landing on soft grass. After a brief examination, I gave her pain-relieving injections. I had to take off my rope so I could move about, but the height did not worry me that much because I used to go rock climbing. The woman was conscious all the time and kept talking to me, however, most of what she said was not understandable, although she did actually ask me to push her off the ledge to complete her fall.'

Later, she emphasised that she was conscious during her fall and knew the moment she had landed on the ledge because it was so painful. She went on to say she was sorry that she had not succeeded this time and she would try again. She said to Dr R Maggs, 'I had heard of Beachy Head when in Norfolk' to which he commented, 'I wonder whether there is anyone who has not heard of it'.

An Amazing Escape

The next escape, a most incredible one, was in July 1978, near Gun Gardens, when a 29-year-old woman fell almost 90m (300 ft) down the cliff before crashing into a small clump of shrubs growing on a ledge 45m above the beach.[4]

She had travelled to Eastbourne and asked where she could catch the bus to Beachy Head. She was directed to the Pier and there boarded a bus, paying a 5p fare. She said she remembered thinking, 'How strange, it costs just 5p to eternity.'

When she walked across the cliff top towards the edge, she saw an old woman with two little girls, so she decided to wait until they had moved away.

She remembered clearly tumbling down the steep slope. 'Funny way to say it, but it felt like when you were a child rolling over and over down a grassy slope. I remember every minute.' She described how a tiny bush broke her fall and held her, swaying above the hard boulders and shingle on the shoreline.

The alarm was raised at about 1500h when holidaymakers saw her lying on a ledge and reported to the police that she was moving.

When the Chief Coastguard, Garry Russell, reached her, her thoughts were 'Oh God, I can't even do this properly, I am still alive. It was painful, but only really bad when I drew on the cigarette the coastguard offered me which he had rolled with one hand.'

Coastguards Garry Russell and Barry Lee took her up the cliff face within 45 minutes of the rescue commencing. Dr Rew, the Police Surgeon, who had also been lowered to administer emergency treatment, said, 'I must admit I was just a little tired after the rescue and a bit out of breath. Generally the whole operation went well and I had no real fears. I was just anxious to get down to the casualty as soon as possible.' Garry Russell agreed, 'I was surprised to find her alive. She was in great pain.' He also admitted that he had decided not to wait for his full complement of coastguards to reach the site, but went over the cliff when only two of his team of ten were in place. 'It was an emergency and I could not wait, but most of them had arrived by the time I reached her.' During the rescue her husband reached the scene. After treatment in the ambulance, she was rushed to hospital. Aside from general scratches and bruises she had fractures of both legs and both arms but, surprisingly, no serious head or trunk damage.

She went on to say that she was sorry for what she had done and felt she had let her doctors down, 'But I am better for the experience, now I feel that I have thought it through, and my daughter is a reason for living.

'I have a very painful right shoulder and my left wrist is sore when moved. Only really bad the next day when I thought I was dying, but that was only letting all my pains and aches get on top of me.'

She was in hospital till the end of August and needed crutches for walking six months later when she said, 'I feel my life was saved for some purpose. I don't know yet what, but I believe I will know one day and I shall never try to end my life again.' She urged those contemplating suicide to ring the "Samaritans" using the telephone box at Beachy Head, put up in 1976 for use by people in distress.

'I discovered so many good friends; the surgeon who saved my legs, the nurses and others of the hospital staff and the wonderful WRVS ladies, I want to thank them all from the bottom of my heart. I feel I owe it to all these people that I should never try to throw away my life again.'

Asked her why she tried Beachy Head, she replied, 'I had tried everything else. It is not even as if I like heights, I cannot stand on a chair at home to reach to a shelf.'

It must be said that although she dropped some 90m she had not chosen the most precipitous part of the cliff, but one where there is a succession of slopes. Even so, she was lucky not to sustain more severe injuries during the fall, and it was quite by chance that, instead of a final vertical drop, she became caught up in a bush and her fall arrested.

In 1979, almost exactly a year after her fall, she was again contemplating catching the bus to the cliff, 'But when in hospital I had been visited by Garry Russell who made me promise that I would never get into that state again without telephoning him. I suddenly remembered my promise and telephoned him'. After a talk with Mr Russell she said, 'Life did not seem so bad any more.' Mr Russell would only confess, 'I just didn't want to go down after her again.'

A truly amazing escape and recovery. In 1981 she still had sciatica and limitation of some back and leg movements, but is alive and well in the 1990s.

Dr Rew being lowered down the cliff to assist a woman trapped on a ledge

The summer of 1979 saw two more astounding escapes. In the first a frail 73-year-old lady survived a 75m (250 ft) fall, and in the other a middle-aged woman lived despite a near 55m (180 ft) fall and lying unconscious on a ledge afterwards for nearly 30 hours.

The pensioner who survived the 75m fall on Monday, 25 June 1979, came from Polegate, near Eastbourne.[5] A widow, she was seen to fall over the cliff near Whitbread Hollow by a group who were picnicking on the beach below. She tumbled down the irregular cliff face until caught up on a ledge about 15m above the beach. The picnickers raised the alarm and two policemen climbed up the cliff to comfort the woman until Dr Rew could be lowered down the cliff to give her treatment. After he had examined her he decided it would be best if she was lifted to the top in the cliff stretcher rather than lowered to the beach, much to the chagrin of the ambulance team waiting below. As mentioned, beach conveyance is often a stressful, jolting journey, whereas once victims are lifted to the cliff top they can be transported rapidly to hospital. She was admitted to a local hospital with fractures along with multiple abrasions.

She said, 'Hopeless isn't it? Often said I would go over Beachy Head. Very painful, I have nobody in the world. I want to talk to people and they don't want to talk to me'.

She was an ill lady who had suffered a minor stroke a few months earlier.

"I Just Kept Walking"

Within a month of this tragic story a 48-year-old Brighton woman had a miraculous escape after falling 55m.

Again, instead of plummeting to her death at the foot of the cliffs, she landed on a ledge, little more than two metres wide, her fall broken by scrub and bushes.[6]

She had decided to end her life because of business worries. Having made her decision she hailed a taxi outside the railway station at Eastbourne and told the driver to take her to Beachy Head "where people jump off"; as she said later, 'Believe it or not he did. I was in a bit of a state and if I had been the taxi driver, I would have driven to the nearest police station or hospital, but he dropped me at a telephone box up there because I wanted to call my daughter. I kept some coins for the call, gave him the contents of my purse and told him, "Keep the rest - I won't need them." Then he drove off. I telephoned my daughter, started off walking and just kept walking. I do not remember seeing the cliff edge or going over.'

The ledge which halted her fall was the only one on that stretch of cliff and she lay on it unconscious through a chilly night until the following day. On that Monday afternoon, 16 July, a party of day trippers from Brighton spotted her part of the way down the cliff when they were walking at Gun Gardens.

The alerted Garry Russell and his team began the rescue operation, in the course of which an ambulance man and Deputy Police Surgeon, Dr Nicholas Sargant, were lowered down the cliff face to give treatment. Holidaymakers gathered to watch the rescue drama and after the injured woman had been strapped to a stretcher and winched to the cliff top, she was rushed by helicopter (from RAF Manston) to a local hospital.

Reviewing the story, it appears that she fell at 0930h on the morning of 15 July and it was not until 1530h on 16 July that she reached the hospital.

She was discharged some weeks later having had treatment for injuries which included fractures of ribs, both legs, a fractured spine, pelvis and wrist, as well as bruises and lacerations to the head and neck.

'I came round with an oxygen mask over my face. The doctors and nurses were marvellous. I am a mess but I am a lucky mess. When I think of all the others who have gone over and not lived it makes me realise how fantastic it is. Three people went over within days of me and they all died.' She went on to say that when she was fully recovered she hoped to become a Samaritan to help other would-be suicides. More than a year later she had loss of memory and, although fully coherent, could not recall the fall.

Two "footnotes" on this incident. In the course of the rescue a thief stole a pair of Garry Russell's shoes which he had left next to the coastguard Land Rover after changing into his rescue gear, and a spokesman for the Eastbourne taxi firms, when asked for his comments on the taxi driver's actions, said, 'If there is anything a bit dicey about a fare we take them to the Police.'

More Escapes

Between February 1982 and April 1984 there were four more escapes, not from as great a height as the last three, but showing further variations in the site chosen and the reasons behind the fall. Unfortunately, they all had long-term effects from their injuries.

On 31 January 1982 a 28-year-old male, an in-patient of a local psychiatric hospital, fell about 20m to be caught on bushes where the cliff is 125m high. The drama started when an ice-cream salesman telephoned the police to say that a man was dangerously near the cliff edge. Police Constables Keith Sillery and Raymond Hills climbed down without ropes to the patient, where they were joined by Garry Russell and a local medical practitioner, Dr Adrian Head, who stayed with the

From the beach the tiny ledge onto which a 73-year-old woman fell in June 1979 appears to be half way up the cliff. Typical terrain at the base of the cliffs

injured man until he could be taken to hospital in a helicopter. The doctor found that the victim was shocked, but fully conscious although later he did lose consciousness for a few minutes.

The injuries included fractures of ribs, breast bone and a leg.

He had attempted suicide previously by cutting his wrists and he had also thrown himself in front of a car - only to land on the bonnet, unhurt.

When asked what happened he said, 'Yes, I jumped and got caught in a hawthorn bush, I wouldn't try again.' To the question why Beachy Head, he replied that he was fed up with the hospital. He was a voluntary patient and could, of course, leave at any time, as he had done for his visit to Beachy Head.[7] He was referred back to his hospital a week later, having behaved in an unruly manner.

A woman of 23 survived a fall to the Whitbread Hollow beach on Thursday, 25 November 1982, where the cliffs are about 35m high. She sustained fractures of her head and left leg, along with soft tissue injuries. She was not fit for discharge until the following March when she still had some restriction of movement.[8]

On 8 September 1983 a 68-year-old woman from South Croydon fell 25m. She was admitted to hospital having sustained a combination of injuries, including fractures of her left leg and a new break in an old fracture of her left hip.

She had a history of attempting suicide before and came to Eastbourne by train, so it was said, "On a one-way ticket".

The last of the four, another 23-year-old, jumped over on Sunday, 15 April 1984 at Holywell. Here the cliffs are less than 30m high and are used only by strangers who must think they have reached the heights of Beachy Head, instead of merely the first cliffs at the end of the Eastbourne promenade. She was unconscious when found and on transfer to hospital she had many scalp and facial lacerations, with fractures of both legs.

Her right side was paralysed and during her first week in hospital she required ventilation in the ITU. Even on discharge more than two months later there was some weakness of the right arm.

She said, 'I did it on an impulse I suppose ...... Won't do it again.' She complained that she was not able to hold down a job, that she didn't like her job, and that, 'I had a bad day so came to Eastbourne.'

Dropping off to Sleep

A further escape was on 1 August 1987, when a 24-year-old man from Poole fell a few metres east of the lighthouse. The exact height of fall was uncertain, but it was over 60m and the injuries included fractures of the left arm, left leg and right collar bone, with further damage to the spine and chest.[9]

He had an obsessive/compulsive disorder which improved with treatment, but always deteriorated after leaving hospital.

He said, 'When it takes four hours to get dressed of a morning, an hour to eat anything and two hours to go to the lavatory, when your parents are getting on and when even the Ministry recognises your situation with an Invalidity Allowance you come to the decision that you have to think of something. I am not depressed - it was just a practical solution. I wanted a method which would cause no trouble to anyone and I chose the highest point on the coast and everyone knows that is Beachy Head.

'I wouldn't do it again because it has caused trouble and it is evident that it is not guaranteed successful. I hadn't got the nerve to jump over so I took sleeping tablets and sat on the edge in such a position that when I dosed off I would fall over. I think it was about half an hour before I fell.'

The next year a 30-year-old woman, an inpatient at a psychiatric hospital, 'just walked over to the left of the lighthouse' on 4 March 1988. On this occasion the Police were alerted by Bernard Dyer, ex-PC and now a local taxi driver, who saw her walk towards the edge rather than to the Beachy Head pub.[10] She said she was fed up with life and, when asked why Beachy Head, she replied, 'I couldn't think of any other way - can you suggest another method?'

Three months afterwards a 38-year-old Irish builder sustained a fractured arm and leg following an accident in June 1988, when he said part of the cliff edge collapsed, throwing him some 25m down the slopes.

All these survivors fell east of the lighthouse, most did not jump, but slid off, and they either landed on a grassy bank or fell less than 35 metres.

Dogs also have their escapes as when *Jasper,* a black Labrador, fell over the cliff near Gun Gardens on 26 June 1985. The dog plunged 90m before crashing on to a ledge, still 30m short of the beach. Garry Russell, who was lowered to the rescue, said, 'It was pretty hard getting him up. He must have weighed 40 pounds.' When taken to a local vet *Jasper* was found to have a dislocated hip and cuts.[11]

It could be said that some of the most miraculous "escapes" have been when a fall has been narrowly avoided or prevented.

On 22 February 1977 a musician from a local Country Club missed death by a fraction when at 0400h his car left the road near Cow Gap and came to rest with its front wheels over the edge, just above a 90m drop. The 19-year-old driver, knocked unconscious in the crash, recovered and rang the police station. The police reached the scene and took the driver to a local hospital. They found the windscreen of the car pushed out and papers and sheet music strewn around, with tyre marks leading from the road and swerving crazily from side to side down a track leading through gorse to the cliff edge. The car was towed away and the driver allowed home from hospital later the same day.[12]

Another motorist had a narrow escape when his car plunged down a steep embankment near Whitbread Hollow on Thursday, 28 February 1980. The 23-year-old from Reigate drove the Hillman *Hunter* car over a hummock, opposite the car park, and was only brought to a halt about 30m down the hillside by a dense growth of gorse bushes.

A man, walking his dog, heard the car engine and noticed the beige coloured back of the car, otherwise hidden in the thick undergrowth. He called the police who conveyed the driver to a local hospital where he was treated for shock and cuts and subsequently transferred to a hospital in Surrey.[13]

There are evidently as many varieties of "an escape" as of "a fall". Some even manage to help themselves, such as a 12-year-old boy who attempted a climb near Cow Gap on 25 February 1972. He reached about 50m and thought himself stranded. In a panic he called for help, but before he could be reached, he managed to slither down to safety all in one piece, all by himself.

Yet another "escape" with a difference happened on Sunday morning, 13 July 1980, when a 21-year-old Hove student drove his car to the edge of the cliffs at Belle Tout - where a Brighton woman had driven over only two months before.

He scrambled clear of the car, unhurt, leaving it balanced precariously with both front wheels over the edge. He next walked a mile to the telephone box near the Beachy Head Hotel and requested emergency assistance from the Royal Automobile Club's headquarters at Croydon. The RAC operators kept him talking while the police were alerted and two patrol cars were sent to investigate.[14]

An RAC patrolman prevented the blue Fiat *Strada* car from tipping over the cliff by roping it to his own vehicle until a recovery truck arrived. The police afterwards explained that they were treating the incident as a social problem, but sadly the student returned to jump over the cliff three months later.

Surely, however, the most unbelievable "escape without a fall" was that of the 23-year-old teacher whose husband confessed to seven attempts to kill her while she remained blissfully unaware of his murderous campaign. One of the methods to which he admitted was an attempt to push his wife off Beachy Head.[15]

The answer, therefore, to the original question, must be that it is possible to survive certain falls at Beachy Head, but not often, and it's not to be relied upon.

8 BEACHY HEAD GOES TO WAR

Many older people will recall the web of vapour trails against the blue sky over Beachy Head in August and September 1940. This was evidence of the Battle of Britain being fought above, but Beachy Head has witnessed many other stirring moments in British history and was used as a vantage point for earlier battles.

In Saxon times, the Danes and other pirates who raided here were described as "sea wolves that live on the pillage of the world."[1] William of Normandy (before he conquered) used it as a mark to navigate his fleet in September 1066. In 1342, during the reign of Edward III, more than half the standing crops were destroyed by French raiders and, about this time, an iron gate was fitted into the narrow defile of Birling Gap. It was so in 1587 when, with the Great Armada imminent, the surveyors of coast defence orders recommended "that Byrlinge Gappe is either to be fortified or ramed uppe. We hold yt beste to be ramed uppe. And so betwene Cuckmer and Borne no landing place to entre uppon the mayne."

The Battle of Beachy Head

A full scale, if not so successful, battle would have been observed from Beachy Head in 1690 when the combined English and Dutch fleets were defeated by the French, three leagues (about ten miles) south of Beachy Head. This would be near to-day's light-tower.

The English call it "The Battle of Beachy Head" fought on the 30 June and the French "Beveziers" [or Pevensey] on the 10 July - they were using different calendars. The French fleet under Tourville had 73 ships of the line, plus 18 fire ships, totalling 4702 pieces of cannon, whereas the English could only muster 35 ships, plus 16 fire ships and the Dutch 22 ships and 4 fire ships, with a combined ordnance of 3816. In other accounts MA Lower and AR Hope Moncrieff say there were 82 French ships and 56 English and Dutch; while JD Parry says 78 French were against 56 English and Dutch.

Whatever, the French had superior numbers and King William, who was in Ireland, had merely 7000 troops for the defence of the country, so the English Admiral, Arthur Herbert, Earl of Torrington, convinced of the dire consequences of a severe defeat, wanted to avoid an engagement. The Privy Council, however, ordered, "...you should upon any advantage of ye wind give battle to ye Enemy..."

Parry describes it as, "A not very usual tale to tell when speaking of English naval history". Action began about 0900h when the Dutch attacked the French van with success while the English Blue Squadron engaged the French rear, but the Red Squadron in the centre could not reach the others which caused a gap between them and the Dutch. The French surrounded the Dutch, who though defending themselves with great bravery, suffered from the unequal contest. Eventually, Torrington, in his flagship the *Royal Sovereign,* drove between the

Dutch and French and anchored when it became calm at 1700h. Finding the Dutch and English fleets were too impaired to renew the action he retired with the flood tide. The French pursuit continued as far as Rye, the *Anne* had to be run ashore and burnt at Winchelsea and three Dutch vessels went aground.

Jean Bart had reconnoitred the coast well for the French and their superior firepower told on the day. The Dutch lost three ships, and the English two ships and 350 men, but although the French harried ships stranded at Pevensey, they were hampered by perverse winds, and had to abandon the chase. [2, 3, 4, 5, 6]

The French had been at sea since the end of May and by the time they returned to Brest, on 5 August, 8 800 seamen (one third of their manpower) had to be put ashore with scurvy and other illnesses and the French were obliged to lay up their fleet. When they put to sea again in 1692 French seapower was effectively destroyed by Torrington at the Battle of La Hogue.

The Wish Tower Museum, mentioned in Chapter 1, displayed a cannon ball (about the size of a tennis ball) which the founder of the museum, Harry Hollobon, said he found in the cliff under Beachy Head. It is unlikely that it came from any of the ships in the main action, though it is just possible that it came from a ship engaged in the pursuit that followed.

Actions against the French continued in these waters although more in the way of skirmishes. In 1706 a French squadron under the corsair Duquay Trouin captured two English men-of-war and their convoy off Birling Gap and, as already referred to by Parson Darby, a French force landed west of Birling Gap, terrorised the populace and stole their cattle.

It is recorded that the people of Eastbourne lined up on the cliff top to watch a Christmas Day fight off Beachy Head in 1778 between the *Greyhound,* carrying 10 four-pounder guns and 25 crew, and a French cutter, of 14 six-pounders and 120 men, which was attempting to capture five colliers creeping along the coastline from Newcastle to Portsmouth. A favourite pastime of the French at this time was to divert English colliers because of the prohibition of coal exports to France. The *Greyhound* had been making for Newhaven, but put about on hearing the cutter's shots and although out-gunned, fought in the way a terrier fights a bull, to such good effect that there was time for the colliers to escape and for two other English ships to escort the French cutter to Hastings. The *Greyhound* limped into Newhaven, having sustained over 200 hits and with half her crew dead or dying, following her successful action.[7]

The Napoleonic Wars

In August 1793, artillerymen camped on Beachy Head for an ordnance survey heard the cries of the crew of an English brig boarded by a French privateer under Beachy Head. They were unable to help because they did not have any cannon.

Perhaps as a result of this episode we have the feature known as Gun Gardens. The site name probably relates to military ordnance at the time of Napoleon.

Gun Gardens was the nearest cliff top to the Coastguard Station (see Chapter 4) and is illustrated in SL Johnson's panoramic map of Eastbourne and neighbourhood in the Towner Museum. Reference is made to, "...the grassy hollow called Gun Garden where...a gun was planted at the time of the French war, and there was also a spot known as Gun Hole immediately below the Coastguard Station".[8]

Great activity was seen near here during Napoleonic times - in September 1811 *HMS Hermes* rammed a French privateer underneath Beachy Head - but most military works were along the beaches, where the Martello Towers and Langney Forts had been erected. It is recorded, however, that on 1 November 1804 the Sussex Militia, encamped "near the bleak summit of Beachy-head", took part in a grand sham fight before striking camp and marching off to Colchester. An 1806 report states that the Eastbourne garrison of the Sussex Militia will "leave this place to encamp on the sunny summit of Beachy on Wednesday next".[9]

Beachy Head was a witness, if only vicariously, of another great sea battle. In October 1904, Admiral Sir Geoffrey Miles, then a 14-year-old schoolboy, was walking on Beachy Head and saw the Russian Imperial Baltic Fleet under Admiral Rozhdestvensky steaming down the English Channel on its way to annihilation by the Japanese in the Tsushima Strait on 28 May 1905.

The First World War

Eastbourne continued as a holiday town during 1914-18. There were no evacuees, and the populace were reminded of the war by the casualty lists, the convalescent "Boys in Blue", and the distant booming of the guns in France.

The Channel was exceptionally busy as ships criss-crossed, ferrying millions of troops to and from France. There were many sinkings off the Head, some undoubtedly due to enemy action, but details were not always released because of wartime censorship, for example, the cargo ship, *Carlisle Castle,* and the *UB 130* were sunk off Beachy Head.[10]

The *Vesuvio* blew up near Beachy Head on 6 April 1916. Whatever the cause, either a mine or torpedo, within ten minutes the vessel had gone, but 15 survivors were rescued by a Royal Naval patrol boat. The Eastbourne lifeboat rescued crew from both the ss *Cairntorr* in March 1915 and the *Alaunia* in October 1916.

The *Ushla,* an Italian tramp steamer, was stranded below Bailey's Brow of the Seven Sisters in November 1916. She remained below the cliffs until broken up in 1928. In a fascinating twist to the tale, on 15 April 1919 the *UB121,* one of two submarines being towed to Cherbourg as part of German war reparations to France, slipped her tow and came ashore at the very same spot, jamming her bow into the remains of the *Ushla's* engine room.

HMS Ariadne, an 11 000-ton cruiser minelayer, was torpedoed by a U-boat four sea miles off Eastbourne on 26 July 1917 with the loss of 38 lives. The tanker *Mira* sank about three miles off Cuckmere Haven on 11 October 1917, and five weeks later the *Lalen Mendi,* a Spanish steamship, sank six miles off Eastbourne.

Perhaps the most dramatic wartime disaster on the Downs happened in December 1917. During the 1914-18 war, anti-submarine patrols were operated by small airships. They first flew from Polegate aerodrome in July 1915 using Submarine Scout (SS) class and Coastal class airships, replaced in 1917 by SSZ types.

The U 121 and the Ushla *lying side by side at the base of the cliffs in 1919*

On 22 December the weather was fine and several airships were out. About 1500h, however, a thick fog developed and the ships were ordered to return. They could not land at Polegate, so two descended near the Coastguard station at Beachy Head and two on the Downs near Jevington. In the course of the evening a wind blew up which, while lifting the fog at Polegate, increased the danger to the exposed airships. Instructions were given to return and the two airships at Beachy Head started off.

It was now dark with mist and the SSZ7, looking for the aerodrome lights, discerned an Aldis signal lamp below and dropped down, thinking it had reached Polegate. Before the pilot discovered that the light was from the SSZ10, one of the craft still moored at Jevington, his airship ripped the envelope fabric of the SSZ10 below him and set fire to the escaping hydrogen. The blazing SSZ7 shot into the air and crashed into the snow. Lt Swallow, pilot of the SSZ7 was killed, but two severely injured aircrew, Mechanics Hughes and Dodd, were extricated despite exploding bombs which amputated an arm of one of their rescuers. Albert Medals were awarded to Lieutenant VA Watson and Mechanics HV Robinson and EE Steere for their part in the rescue.[11]

An anti-submarine airship coming in to land at Polegate aerodrome

The Second World War

The war started early at Beachy Head. On August Bank Holiday 1939, an RAF Bristol Blenheim bomber on exercises from Wattisham, crashed into the cliff in heavy ground mist, killing the crew of three and a young woman who happened to be walking on the cliffs.

This tragedy apart, Eastbourne and around commenced the war as a Safe Area and thousands of evacuees descended on the town from London.

Early in the war all we have is a report that a U-boat was sunk about two miles off Beachy Head, but you can still see part of the ss *Barnhill* bombed off Beachy Head on 20 March 1940. A 5000-ton vessel, she was set on fire and drifted ashore east of Eastbourne. The locals, on rations, were pleased when part of its cargo of tinned foods drifted ashore.[12] The boilers can be seen, at low Spring Tides, near the entrance to the new Marina (see Chapter 3, Shipwrecks and Lifeboats). A few months later the Eastbourne lifeboat went to Dunkirk, along with other local craft.

In June 1940, with the Germans only 65 miles away across the Channel, Eastbourne and Beachy Head suddenly found themselves in the Front Line, the first bombs fell on 7 July 1940, a U-boat evened matters up by shelling the town and Cuckmere Haven on 31 August, and most of the inhabitants were evacuated.

For the rest of the war civilian access to the area was restricted, the beaches had obstructions to stop aircraft landing, and bathing was forbidden. Concrete blocks, termed "Dragon's Teeth", were used to block road junctions as anti-tank defences. Mostly removed by 1956,[13] a few can still be seen at East Dean.

Beachy Head saw great activity. In 1940 it was termed the "Clapham Junction of the Air," used by both German and Allied navigators.

Wartime poster, "Your Britain fight for it now", showing Belle Tout, Birling Manor, and a shepherd, his dog and sheep {Imperial War Museum}

The first enemy aircraft brought down near Beachy Head was a Messerschmitt 110. It fell in Meads on the afternoon of 16 August 1940, killing the pilot, but the gunner, Richard Schurk, parachuted into the sea near Holywell. His parachute had collapsed over his head, and a boat put out from a nearby minesweeper, but when the crew heard from watchers on the shore that the parachutist was not British they turned and went back to their ship.[14]

Two German airmen in a rubber dinghy came safely ashore near Beachy Head on 7 September 1940, after drifting for 16 hours.

Emergency airfields were constructed along the coast, mainly grass with any dips filled with rubble. One was at Friston, just inland of the Seven Sisters. On 7 July 1941 it was used by Wg/Cdr Douglas Bader's 616 Squadron to escort bombers to Northern France. The Operation Record Book states, "A new airfield just lately completed near Beachy Head. This proved unsatisfactory for landing owing to small size and uneven surface and one of our pilots crashed his aircraft there".[15]

Even so, a Sgt Smith of 616 Squadron put down there four days later and was refuelled on his way back to Tangmere, and many bombers just managed to make it and belly-flop on the grass. In the course of the war and in poor weather others weren't so fortunate, including a C47 which crashed near the hotel,[16] a Flying Fortress at Willingdon, another American aircraft in the sea near Holywell, and a transport Dakota downed at Wilmington in February 1945 when 23 died.

After the Battle of Britain the area around Beachy Head was subjected to intermittent day and night raids until 1942 when the Germans switched to "hit and run" tactics.

Fighter bombers would sweep in over the coast, drop bombs, and machine-gun the town and any small craft out at sea. These raids caused numerous casualties and were particularly frightening because the planes could be over the coast before any warning. It was said the fighters switched off their engines to glide in, but the German fighters were unable to restart their engines in the air. What happened was that they flew in low, at speed, often over Birling Gap, and were not heard approaching until they boosted their engines to zoom away.[17] In time a local warning was devised, called the "Cuckoo" after the sound it made.

Over 1943-44 there was sporadic night bombing, and from June to August 1944 Beachy Head experienced V1 bombardment.

British and Canadian troops swarmed over the area. Their Churchill tanks, stationed under the trees in Meads, clattered up to the Downs each morning to churn up the turf. They were no respecters of property; damage to garden gates and walls was commonplace and five lamp-posts were demolished in one night.

King George VI visited the Armoured Division on 13 May 1942; in the July a tank under repair ran out of control over the Beachy Head cliffs, killing the driver.

During the Battle of Britain the "Few" communicated with Biggin Hill and Tangmere by radio telephone. These sets only had a range of about 100 miles, so for sorties over the French coast Forward Relay Stations were established at Beachy Head. By this time Beachy Head also had radio vans which took a compass bearing on any transmission, especially useful for tracking pilots in difficulties. As James D Lewis says, "...fighter pilots were notoriously late in sending out a distress call...often all [that] was heard was '...Mayday, Mayday, Mayday, Tulip Red One, am diving into the drink' - lasting perhaps four seconds". The moment the position of the plane was fixed, high speed launches sped out from Newhaven to pick up the pilot. At the time of the 19 August 1942 combined amphibious raid on Dieppe (co-ordinated from Eastbourne), 21 calls were received from members of the air umbrella who had to ditch, and air-sea rescue saved 19. Typhoon fighters covering the Dieppe operation had formed up over Beachy Head.

The Germans had their own air-sea rescue scheme first in 1940, but the Beachy Head one became so successful that the Germans began sending out false bearings to confuse the limping aircraft, so the radio intelligence station soon put a stop to that. They also plotted the positions of all the German radar stations along the French coast so that the fighter bombers knew where to attack, and thanks to them it was possible to mount the famous commando attack on the Wimera radar station, when the installation was spirited back to Britain.

The first Direction Fixing equipment was set up in a mobile van near to the dew pond on Warren Hill in March 1941 and later in a hut nearer the East Dean Road. The RAF ran the radar and the Royal Observer Corps the Observer Post. Many WAAF were stationed at Beachy Head, and there was even a Royal Naval Signal Station on Willingdon Hill.

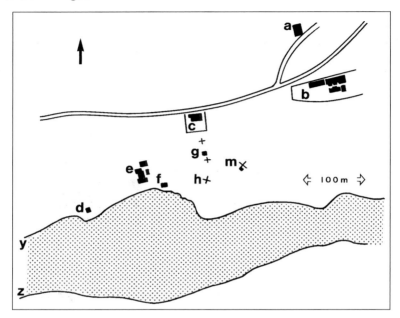

The Radar and Observer posts on top of Beachy Head in 1942. The Beachy Head Hotel is marked "a", the Signal Station "b", the Signalman's hut "c", a CD No 1 Mk IV is "d", the CHL building "e", a type II set "f", RT/WT equipment "g", a wireless beacon "h", and an IFF interrogator mast and hut "m". The cliff top is marked "y", and "z" is the high water mark

The secret war was in force at Beachy Head. Within a few months of the outbreak of war both the army and navy had small radar stations concealed on the cliff edge. They were referred to as CHL stations [Chain Home Link], working in association with bigger stations elsewhere.

One sideline was that German TV pictures from Paris could be picked up at the Beachy Head monitoring station between July 1942 and August 1944.

During the later years of the war, transmitter and receiver vans were parked all over the Downs; they included some from the US Air Force. An Air Ministry ground control interception radar network, under Squadron Leader "Bill" Igoe, controlled all the "air sweeps" crossing the Channel from an operations room at Beachy Head, which was also involved in the interception of over 500 enemy aircraft, and played its part in the destruction of more than 550 V1 flying bombs.

As early as 11 May 1941 the Beachy Head installations were bombed, and the following year, on 23 May, a strafing Me 109 was shot down near Black Robin Farm. The 23-year-old pilot, described by local farmer's wife, Eileen Goldsmith, as looking about 18, escaped uninjured.[18] Other Me 109s weren't so lucky, falling into the sea, but one made a forced landing near the A259 on 30 September 1940.

In the latter years of the war it was a common happening for the Observer post and other units on Beachy Head to be shot up by FW190 fighter/bombers.

Many famous air aces, such as Douglas Bader and Paddy Finucane, received their instructions from the Beachy Head units, which also controlled the Beaufighter and Mosquito night fighters - and the Lysanders which were used to penetrate deep into France on SOE missions. Some nights as many as 12 of these aircraft would cross the channel, at this stage in radio silence, and only as they returned, or in some cases about to crash, were their transmitters switched on.

On 16 April 1943, Spitfires of 403 Squadron flew out from and returned by Beachy Head for a raid on Le Harve.

German TV test card picture from Paris picked up by the Beachy Head detectors during the 1939-45 war {M Ockenden}

The Beachy Head installations were part of the massive aerial array which, in June 1944, blasted away any German interference and provided radio cover for the fleet of assault landing craft, and later during the bitter battle for Caen.[19] Almost all the equipment had been dismantled before VE Day in May 1945, and to-day there is nothing to see of the aerials and masts. The last remains of the wartime RAF radar station were demolished on 16 October 1963.

Evidence of the consequences of war was not only bomb sites and rationing, but more poignantly the bodies of unknown seamen washed ashore at Birling Gap.

A number are buried in East Dean and Friston churchyards, their headstones well maintained by the War Graves Commission.

On 1 December 1943, HM trawler *Aventurine* sank about one mile south of Beachy Head, and the *U 413,* which had sunk the destroyer *HMS Warwick* with the loss of 68 lives in 1944, was itself later destroyed off Beachy Head.

The Belle Tout lighthouse had a hard war, looking from the landward side in 1945

It was from Beachy Head on the still clear night of 12/13 June 1944 that the rocket exhaust of the first Vl flying bomb (or Doodlebug) was sighted 30 miles away: it fell near Haywards Heath at 0420h. The vertical cliff face was hit by V1s on both 23 and 27 June, and one fell on the Beachy Head Downs on 6 August 1944. Most flying bombs that fell around Beachy Head had been damaged or deflected from their London target. No V2 rockets landed on Beachy Head.

Did the American bandleader Glenn Miller die 30 miles off Beachy Head on 15 December 1944? He went missing on a flight to France, and there is a strong possibility that his Norseman aircraft flew amidst a stream of bombs which were being jettisoned into the sea by Lancaster bombers returning from an aborted raid.[20]

The Cold War and Path to Peace

After the 1939-45 war Britain was at the centre of the cold war and defensive measures were in order. In 1950 an underground radar bunker was built at Beachy Head and became operational by 1953. It closed down in 1957, when new aircraft and nuclear technology made it obsolete. The guardroom, at the entrance, later became the police stables and coastguard building.

The 260-foot long underground operations chamber, which runs beneath the Downs at Beachy Head, was coated in 10-foot thick concrete, and designed to resist atomic and gas attacks. It was to function as a nerve centre in a nuclear war.

The first mention of turning it into a visitor information centre came in 1985. By 1988 local councillors were proposing its conversion into a £3m museum, as a showpiece of wartime artefacts and natural history.[21] Councillors visited the site with representatives of local societies. After squeezing through an entrance hole the size of a manhole in the floor of the coastguard building [now demolished], the party toured the bunker.

Cllr Maurice Skilton said, 'Developing the bunker would be a great boost to the town's tourist industry. As far as the Council are concerned they are most anxious to have a museum.

'There is a lot of scope for the topic of the museum, which could be about the Battle of Britain, or the natural history of Beachy Head'. He went on, 'I have been in touch with groups throughout the country who are most interested in restoring these radar bunkers'.

Barry Cain, who hosted the tour, said, 'There are not many of these stations about as most of them have been filled in. It had a personnel level of up to 200, although only 100 would work there at any one time'.

With the recession the underground museum project didn't get off the ground.

Hidden bunkers are not the only remnants of the war. Even years afterwards there is danger as implements of war turn up. On 26 May 1977 a wartime phosphorus bomb was found by a school party at Cuckmere Haven and exploded when touched, slightly burning two of the teachers. On 10 June 1980 the Downs Ranger, PC Ian Tubb, found 80 four-inch shells in the cliffs when searching for a missing student, and in February 1986 the bomb squad from *HMS Vernon* destroyed 21 unexploded shells. In Garry Russell's words, 'They're not in good condition, being there so long, but they are still dangerous'. As recently as 12 August 1987 six unexploded wartime shells were found below Gun Gardens by coastguards Ivor Pollard and Chris Turner.[22]

In contrast, and in what we all trust is the way ahead, on Easter Monday 1987 Mr Leslie Mason, Eastbourne's Mayor, opened the Beachy Head Peace Path, a tarmac surface for visitors to admire the views in safety. It was dedicated to the UN International Year of Peace.[23]

Three hundred years after the Battle of Beachy Head the 140m cliffs at Gun Gardens provide watchers on the cliffs with the most entrancing and peaceful views of the "new" lighthouse.

Once again, in June 1988, the sound of Spitfires echoed over Beachy Head as their vapour trails wove intricate patterns. This time, happily, they had been hired in a re-enactment for the film *A Piece of Cake*.

9 NATURAL HISTORY

Parry tells the story of three sailors, stranded on Beachy's rocks during a gale in 1821, who found samphire *(Crithmum maritimum)* growing on the rocks. Knowing that rock samphire will not grow under salt water, they could be sure that the rock they were on would not be submerged by the tide and they were safe: a practical use of nature knowledge. It is remarkable how samphire (sea spinach) can survive salt spray, along with wild cabbage and seakale. Mentioned by Shakespeare, it grew luxuriantly according to Lower, writing in the 1860s.[1]

It might not be so abundant now, but all wild life has good years and bad. Not all the plants and animals mentioned will be seen. Some (such as house martins) are seasonal, some (eg. badgers) only appear at night, others are rarely seen and in some years are not to be found.

One example of change is in the number of fish caught. There were regular seasons for certain fish. Autumn would be the herring season, winter was for sprats, in summer the mackerel shoals came along the Channel, and in spring, summer and autumn there were always lobsters and crabs. In the 19th century upwards of 30 boats fished from Eastbourne, now there are less than half-a-dozen, and the shoals have gone.

Samphire

On the other hand, as the *Sussex County Magazine* of 1934 says, the green woodpecker was absent and the magpie rare on the Downs about 1900, but both were common by the 1930s, and the comma butterfly tells much the same story.[2] At the end of the century the green woodpecker has maintained its numbers while the magpie is in such excess that smaller birds are seriously harassed.

Climbing up from the Meads district of Eastbourne on the start of the South Downs Way, you get a hint of the natural splendour. A swath of short turf, from the nibbling of many sheep and rabbits, and a mixture of wild flowers - cowslips in early spring (now no longer collected by the local girls to throw at the Spring Fair) followed by orchids, and later the harebells, bellflowers, viper's bugloss and pheasant's eye. Unless it becomes overgrown, the good old Downland turf is rich in plants with an estimated 46 species per square metre.

For obvious reasons the precise location of some plants is not given, and readers are reminded that it is an offence to pick the wild flowers.

In some ways the Beachy Head Downs remain as unspoilt as at any time, with the same extent of open grassland as thousands of years ago, when there were many Bronze age settlements here, of which traces are still visible around the look out summit of Belle Tout.

Foxes, badgers, adders, grass snakes, slow worms, and common lizards may be found, and although from 1955 to 1975 precious few rabbits were seen following the myxomatosis epidemic they are back in numbers. The adders, which are best avoided, just as they will do their best to avoid you, are found around stones and in pits. If you see a snake swimming, it is usually a harmless grass snake. The slow worm is really a lizard without legs. Other animal life includes moles and hedgehogs (although seldom seen until run over), fox cubs in the hedges, grey squirrels, brown rats, and mice, voles and shrews, providing food for stoats and weasels. Bats, especially pipistrelles, are common in the evening.

The Downland turf is a result of thin soil and deficient nutriments with sheep grazing over hundreds of years. Sheep graze closer than cattle and prefer shorter grass. This allows the development of short, springy grassland, which has seldom if ever been ploughed. They were Southdown sheep, but now are mainly Scottish Blackface and Lakeland Herdwick crosses: other varieties may be seen at Terry Wigmore's Seven Sisters Sheep Centre along the Birling Gap road.

Where over the years there has been arable farming, the tenant farmers have cultivated Kador and Sportsman winter wheat for seed export, Flanders wheat for bread making, Sonya barley for whisky, Flynor and Maris Huntsman for cattle feed. Latterly the yellow flowers of rape have been seen.

Birds

The Sussex Downs were long associated with the wheatear, still a summer visitor with its black and white tail. These ortolans were caught in their thousands by the shepherds who sold them on, for they were considered a delicacy. It is alleged that in the 1650s the Royalist Wilsons, of Bourne (now Compton) Place, regaled Roundheads sent to investigate them with wheatear pie, which gave them time to burn incriminating documents.[3]

In August 1713 John Macky stayed in Eastbourne. He described the shepherd's method of catching "whit-ears" by making a tunnel in the turf, and wrote, '...the top of the hills called the Downs of Sussex...[are]...the finest carpet in the world'.[4] The wheatear's beautiful pale blue eggs are to be seen not far from the lighthouse.

Beachy Head is a staging post for birds on their migrations and records of bird sightings at Beachy Head extend over many years. Plates show the Downs covered with wild fowl in the 18th century and the great bustard used to roam the South Downs in Gilbert White's time. In the 1800s the Cornish chough nested on Beachy Head, kite and honey buzzards were seen, ravens nested there, and the kestrel, known in Sussex as the windhover. The last bustard was shot in 1876 and a pair of stone curlews managed to last into the 1920s.

Observations range from Dr Gideon Mantell, who on 5 June 1820 recorded in his diary, that he "saw a fine specimen of razor bill *(Alea Torda)* that was shot at Beachy Head - it is rare in Sussex", JH Gurney's 1879 description in *Zoologist* of an albino specimen of red necked grebe, to *The Times* report of 3 January 1989 that a crag martin was seen at Beachy Head on 9 July 1988. The same month terns were filmed feeding at Beachy Head for a BBC-1 TV program.

On the cliffs the common gull is not so common and the black-headed gull (white in winter) prefers to be more inland, so the dark grey-winged herring gull is most numerous: it has a red spot on its beak and is sometimes called the sea-mew. It nests on ledges of cliffs, lays 3-4 brownish eggs, and is a voracious and rapacious feeder, but also moves inland in times of storms.[5] Jackdaws, rooks and rock pipits are also found on the cliffs, while fulmar and guillemot visit. It is of interest that the cleaning of diving bird's feathers when clogged with oil was recorded as long ago as 1934.[6]

The joy of listening to the birds is recounted by Arthur Beckett.[7] 'Blackbird, thrush, wren, robin, chaffinch, greenfinch ...a skylark winging its way skyward until both lark and song are lost in the liquid blue.'

It is not unusual to hear the yaffle of a green woodpecker and in springtime the clear call of the cuckoo, coming from Went Hill near Birling Gap, while the wood pigeon is heard throughout the year.[8]

Herring Gull

Other birds which may be seen are the bullfinch, chaffinch, collar dove, field fare, great black-backed gull, lesser black-backed gull, crows, lapwing, linnet, tawny and short-eared owl, pied wagtail, black redstart (at Belle Tout), tree sparrow, flocks of starlings, stonechat, swallows on the telephone wires at Birling Gap in autumn, swift, song thrush, mistle thrush, redwing, great tit, blue tit, coal tit, long-tailed tit, whinchat and greater-spotted woodpecker.

Cuckmere Haven, to the west of Beachy Head, is the site of the Seaford Head Nature Reserve, which provides a mixture of Downland, Wet Pasture and Foreshore habitats. There are footpaths on either side of the Cut. Any stretch of inland water is likely to have mallard, coot (white beak) and moorhen (red beak), but the Wet Pasture has other ducks and waders such as shelduck, ringed plover, dunlin and redshank and flocks of others may be flying off the coast. The foreshore has a wave-cut platform with pools and gullies for many plants and small animals. The rules of the Nature Reserves include no fires, no guns, and keep your dog on a lead if sheep or cattle are grazing.

Birds seen more often around Cuckmere Haven than on the Downs include the curlew, peregrine falcon, greenshank, hen harrier, redstart, common and green sandpipers, shoveler, yellow wagtail, garden warbler, and whitethroat.

There are occasional sightings of many other birds including black kite, Dartford warbler and yellow hammer.

The *Sussex County Magazine* reported that in 1934 swifts were last seen at Cuckmere Haven on 8 September, house martins 2 November and swallows 19 November, which is late.[9] The following spring the wheatear (always one of the first) was first seen on 23 March, the chiffchaff 28 March, and the first swallows 17 April[10] - near enough to Gilbert White's 13th of the month.[11]

Trees, shrubs and flowers

Apart from low, wind-misshapen thorns, trees and shrubs are notable for their absence on top of the Downs, but in the lee and away from the sea many flourish, although you have to travel to the Weald to see oaks. They include ash, cedar, field maple, holly, horse chestnut, cypress and pine families, sycamore, and yew. On the inland slopes of the Downs there used to be many English elms.

In the hedges there is the ubiquitous hawthorn (with its fragrant mayflowers and red berries), blackthorn (white blossomed in spring), bramble, laurel, privets, dead nettles and elderflowers, covered in blackberry, bindweed, bramble and traveller's joy (or old man's beard in autumn), with ivy, white cow parsley, dandelions and yellow alexanders at their feet. It is not unusual to see one side of an evergreen tree or hedge damaged by salt spray, while bellflowers, betony, pink centaury, mauve knapweed, and scabious grow right on the edge of the cliffs, albeit half the size of the same plants a few metres inland.

The dark-blue flowered, round-headed rampion *(phytena orbiculare)* is said to be the pride of Sussex, and the small leaved hare's ear *(bupleurum baldense)* is a scheduled species. Other shrubs and flowering plants include: (yellow) agrimony, aquilegia, black byrony, buttercup, sea and white campion, clover, honeysuckle, knapweed, lady's (yellow) bedstraw, wild gooseberry, gorse, forget-me-not, chalk milkwort, (yellow) ragwort (not popular with rabbits), common speedwell, wild (pale yellow) mignonette, rest harrow, yellow toad flax, bird's-foot trefoil or bacon and eggs, ox-eye daisy, eyebright, poppies at the field edges, yellow primrose, bittersweet, hairy and rosebay willowherb, and scarlet pimpernel. There is burnet, dewberry, dog, dropwort and sweetbriar of the roses, self heal, silverweed, wood-sorrell, dwarf, nodding and carline thistles, thyme, violet, the common, kidney and tufted vetches, wayfaring tree, and (white) yarrow. Orchids include the burnt tip, fly, frog, early purple, the bee (the white form local since 1890), early spider (a scheduled species), spotted and pyramidal.[12]

The Downs are too dry for many fungi except a few puffballs.

Butterflies and moths

The diverse habitats and proximity to the continent mean that insects are well represented, although in some years sightings are few and another year there is an abundance - few people will forget the Seven-spot ladybird plague of 1976 or the hosts of Silver Y moths in autumn 1996. Many species of bees and wasps are seen and heard, and among other insects there are springtails on the cliffs, grey bush crickets at Cow Gap, bloody nosed beetles, and green grasshoppers on the Downs. About 20 of the some 50 species of British butterfly have been seen at Beachy Head. They include many red admirals and cabbage whites, brimstone, meadow/wall browns, chalkhill in August, adonis/holly and small blues, small copper, comma, dark green fritillary, gamekeeper, green hairstreak, orange tip in spring, painted lady which is abundant some years flying over from France, peacock, skipper and small tortoiseshell. The variety *helice* of the clouded yellow has been seen at Holywell.

Around any ponds will be seen mayfly, dragon fly *(Aeshna)*, damsel fly, various water beetles, pond and ram's horn snails, frogs and toads.

Geologically, the Beachy Head area consists of chalk, below which is gault (a clay) and upper greensand (a stone with a greenish sheen, used in St Mary's Church). The layers (or strata) of Upper, Middle and Lower Chalk, and Gault and Greensand are seen on the exposed cliff faces. Chalk, a young rock in geological terms, was formed in the Upper Cretaceous period of around 80-100 million years ago, when reptiles such as the ichthyosaur and dinosaur ruled the earth. Chalk was formed only once in the history of the world when there was a dry climate and a low land surface, it is almost pure calcium carbonate and, unlike other sedimentary rocks (limestone, sandstone, shale), contains little other material.

At Holywell there is Belemnite Marl (earth with fossils), at Cow Gap there is gault, greensand and Chalk Marl, and at Birling Gap there are Coombe Deposits, as described in Chapter 1. Winkle stone, otherwise called Sussex marble, is petrified shells. The Seven Sisters are a series of valleys, now dry, but cut by rivers in the Ice Age. The valley bottoms have partly filled with Coombe Deposits.

From the tip of Beachy Head you can see a ledge of greensand running out under the sea to form a "lagoon" at low tide, and at Holywell a similar ledge runs parallel with the shore to form the Pound.

On the Beach

The boulders on the beaches are usually white chalk, the pebbles are mainly flint (iron impurities colouring them brown and grey), some are fossil sponges, and limestone, apart from the more prosaic wave-polished brick and concrete.

In the rockpools at Holywell, Birling Gap and Cuckmere Haven there are red and green seaweeds, but mostly brown serrated wracks (there is a brown Channel wrack, which readily blackens on drying out), Beadlet and dahlia anemones, shore crabs and, in their shells, hermit crabs are seen, and very rarely squat lobsters.

Most shells are bivalves, such as limpets and razorshells, with a few "snail-like" shells such as whelk. On the few stretches of sand there may be evidence of lugworms and mason worms, and cuttlefish bones (or its shell), whelk egg-cases, and mermaid's purses (the egg-case of dogfish) can be found. At very low tides breadcrumb sponges, prawns and seaslugs may be seen. Fish include rockling, bullhead, goby, blenny and corkwing wrasse. The best month is August.

Just off the beach, pollack, eels and dab can be caught, and further out, especially around old wrecks, bass and beam. Sea bass makes an excellent repast to prepare for a good walk.

10   WALKS AROUND BEACHY HEAD and the SEVEN SISTERS

Between Eastbourne and Seaford is the longest stretch of unspoilt coastline in the South East. Arguably the finest stretch of sea cliffs in Britain, it is well worth the visitor trying to see as much as possible.

These descriptions are just a guide for a stroll on a sunny summer day, you don't need oiled, spiked shoes, although bear in mind that even in warm weather it can be windier and cooler on the Head than the town. Allow half an hour a mile. Do not go walking around Beachy Head in adverse weather conditions or at night.

A bus from Eastbourne front runs to near the Beachy Head Hotel in the summer. There is usually plenty of parking, pay-and-display near the hotel, the hotel has free parking for customers, and on the road to Birling Gap there are further car parks, with free parks near and at the Birling Gap Hotel.

Many paperbacks are on sale in the local shops with detailed walks around Eastbourne, Beachy Head and the Seven Sisters. At Beachy Head, for a pound or two, guided walks are led through the summer by experts such as David Pearce, John Sellers, Phil Luffingham, Graham Parris and David Haizelden. Programs are available at the Countryside Centre.

1.   The Beachy Head Peace Path, about ¹/₂ mile, suitable for wheelchairs.

A tarmac path from just east of the Beachy Head Hotel runs out to near the cliff top and back to west of the hotel. With care all visitors may admire the views of Eastbourne, the old and new lighthouses, and the play of light on the sea, in safety. The path starts and ends near the Downs' purchase seat. Wheelchair access is just across the road from the coach park and lavatories.

2.   Walk around the Beachy Head Hotel, 3 miles.

To the east of the hotel car park is the coastguard and police building, with its prominent aerial, where coastguard rescue material is stored. It used to be on the opposite side of the road near the site of the old Coastguard Station.

Cross over the road, with care, towards the cliffs to the Downs' purchase seat. You can see Eastbourne pier to the left, turn right, cross over the Peace Path to the old Lloyd's watch tower, now a site for a telescope. The concrete supports for the mast in the days of semaphore signalling are visible in the ground.

If you take care and look down from the cliffs near here you will see the red and white-banded lighthouse. To the west is the mound of Belle Tout, with Seaford Head in the background. Looking landwards can be seen medieval banks and ridges in the fields across the road, behind is Bullock Down (a ridge with a double lynchet lane).[1] Just to the left of the banks you can see the marling areas where lime was dug out to be spread over the fields. Such evidence of cultivation extends inland as far as the Combe Hill enclosure area.

Walk down from the Lloyd's Station back across the road and veer to the left over the Downland (which is for your enjoyment) and continue alongside a fence just by the road. As you come to the end of the fence, *Hodcombe* and Belle Tout are ahead. Inland, on Frost Hill, are the remains of a shepherd's hut. Turn right along the line of a fence, part of a medieval boundary, and right again over the first stile. There is an angled flint wall on your left and behind is Sweet Brow barn, sometimes in use by shepherdess Pat Stevens for lambing sheep. To the right a "dew pond" is just visible, depending on the growth of the vegetation. Turn diagonally right through a field which has marl pits and has been sown with Downland wild flowers. This leads back towards the hotel, which has been in sight for most of the walk, where you may wish to dally at the Brewers Fayre.

3. Just around the Beachy Head Hotel, a little sortie.

Cross the road from the children's play area of the hotel, with the telephone kiosk well to your left. You will come to the cut-down Lloyd's watch tower, and continuing to the cliff edge hereabouts the lighthouse is visible from the top of the cliff. Look west to the undulating Downs, Belle Tout, and Cuckmere Haven. Turn left and walk east catching up with the tarmac path to the Downs' purchase seat. Continue along the cliff side of the road with Eastbourne and its pier visible, and Norman's Bay and Hastings beyond. This is a great play area, with kite flying and ball games in progress. Across the road there is a dew-pond just past the far car park. Turn back to the hotel, the red roof of which is in view.

4. Birling Gap Hotel to Beachy Head Hotel, 2½ miles.

From the eastern side of the Birling Gap Hotel carpark turn onto the Downs by the telephone box at the land end of the old coastguard cottages. Take a stepped path and then climb gradually to the old Belle Tout lighthouse. On the way you pass a National Trust cairn. From near the old lighthouse there are lovely views inland of Downland fields, *Cornish Farm* (where Peter Drewett's excavations have revealed exciting finds), and the grey Friston water tower is in the distance.

Encircling Belle Tout are two lines of earthworks, used as footpaths to-day. They are the remains of a fort built in pre-Roman times, the southern half having fallen into the sea. There are similar forts at Seaford Head and Mount Caburn near Lewes. Walk round to the other side of Belle Tout where the new (1902) lighthouse may be glimpsed to the right of the cliffs. If you think you have walked enough, see Walk 5.

Otherwise walk down the Belle Tout access road, go past the lay-by, which is within ten metres of the cliff edge, and continue eastwards by the cliff top. Just inland, converted from farm labourers' dwellings, is *Hodcombe,* which means warm valley; curiously it stands near Frost Hill. Bullock Down, in the mid distance is where hoards of Roman coins have been found. Looking over the cliff edge, just past the point of the headland, the red-banded lighthouse appears to be a toy coming out of the sea.

Continue a gentle undulating climb, past Shooter's Bottom, to the old Lloyd's watch tower, now an octagon of seats with a view, where if you bear to the left the Beachy Head Hotel is on the other side of the road.

5. Birling Gap to Belle Tout and back, 1½ miles.

From the car park of the Birling Gap Hotel, take Walk 4 as far as Belle Tout. On the way back either retrace your steps or take one of the lower trails through the gorse on the right. They have a habit of dying out, but you will find one that takes you down to the NT summer car parks by the side of the road. This was the site of the old Golf Club House. The hotel provides refreshments and accommodation, with John Smiths, Carlsberg and fish specialities.

6. Along the beach between Holywell and Birling Gap, 4 miles.

A sea-level traverse from Eastbourne front to Birling Gap, or vice versa, is possible. The high tides are funnelled along the Channel and at the spring and autumn equinoxes touch 8m (26 ft), but any high tide reaches the cliffs in some places, so check beforehand. Tidetables are available, check that the steps at Birling Gap are open, and don't fall asleep sunbathing half way along.

In practice it is longer than 4 miles and although there are no lines of obstructing rock running out to sea, it is sometimes impossible to avoid getting your feet wet, so sensible shoes/trainers are advised. While the ground can be irregular there is always some beach so long as the tide is right, but it is only for those who are physically able. In the winter of 1855 a wild-duck shooter named Bethel was overtaken by the tide and froze to death on the cliffs.

Just before St Bede's School, near the western end of the parades, cut down a path to the beach, Pinnacle Point is ahead. There are sparkling views of the lighthouse, looking much bigger than from the top of the cliffs, which impress by their sheer - and often overhanging - walls.

At Cow Gap, about a mile further on it is possible to turn inland safely and either turn back to Whitbread Hollow and the Eastbourne front, or gain access to the cliff tops near the Beachy Head Hotel.

The steps at Birling Gap are often removed if damaged by gales, if so an extra two mile walk is involved, under the Seven Sisters cliffs (where again the sea comes up to the cliffs at high tide) to the Cuckmere estuary, and another mile to the road for the bus to Eastbourne. There are refreshments at the Exceat Farmhouse Restaurant (not open every day out of season) and along the A259, across the Cuckmere bridge, is the Golden Galleon pub.

7. East Dean to Birling Gap, 1¼ miles.

Drive along Gilbert's Drive from the A259 at East Dean, there is a free car park about 300m on the right. James Dippery, smuggler uncle of Willard, built one of the houses behind the flint wall. From the Tiger Inn walk across the green and take the upper of the two roads going left. The road goes past the old school and the old bakehouse - with firemarks, one of 1792. (On the right, by a garage, there is a steep concreted path with handrails which leads above the village, and if you haven't much time, go up the steps, along a stone wall, rest for a minute on the memorial seat to Stan Fuller, and after admiring Belle Tout in the distance, look for the mounting steps near the back of the seat, keep right over the stone stile, skirt the trees whose shadows are warped by the folds of the Downs, and go down a lovely field called Hobbs Eares, where the white flint house was built for the Birling Gap telegraphist. You return to East Dean village, entering at the corner of Upper Street and you will soon be back at the green where you started.)

The Went Road continues to an old flint house on the left, *Underhill.* The north east side has bricked-up windows, probably a result of the window tax. The path, known as Went Way, goes over a stile, or gate, and keeping straight on, climbs to the top of Went Hill; along the way there are lovely views of East Dean village, the Saxon church and *Birling Manor.* The two walled fields across the road are called Upper and Lower Dunwick, indicating dairy pasture. The barn just by the *Birling Manor* entrance is called *Dunwick Barn* and is the site of the Seven Sisters Sheep Centre, worth a visit, but not advised at lambing if you are pregnant.

Birling Manor also goes back to Saxon times and after the Norman Conquest was part of the Earl of Mortain's lands, but forfeited to the crown after his son's treason in 1106. After many changes it was purchased by the Davies-Gilbert family. The old Manor House subsequently became a barn and in 1926 the present Bardolf Hall.

The walk continues along a level path before reaching a red-roofed barn on the right. Keep on bearing left down a grassy slope to reach Birling Gap with wonderful views of the sea.

The Seven Sisters

Although not strictly part of Beachy Head, a short reference is made to this contiguous beauty spot.

The Seven Sisters are a series of dry valleys, with the harder chalk rocks forming seven adjacent rounded ridges, between Birling Gap and the Cuckmere estuary. As mentioned, the chalk was formed millennia ago upon the bed of the ocean from the bodies of countless small sea creatures. Later the layers were thrust up by stresses in the earth's crust and about 10 000 years ago the sea flooded in to separate England from the continent, cutting the cliffs as we see them to-day.

The white exposed cliffs of the Seven Sisters represent a fine piece of unspoilt coastline. Their quality was recognised when the Countryside Act of 1968 designated them as an area of Heritage Coast.

All the cliff faces are sheer, especially the three western Sisters, except for an occasional build up of fallen chalk at the base.

The first ridge (or Sister) from the Birling Gap side is called Went Hill Brow locally. It is 45m (146 ft) high (compared with the 165m of Beachy Head). The second Sister is Bailey's Brow at 60m (194 ft). Some say here be a small eighth

Sister, Flat Brow, but Flagstaff Point 47m (153) is truly the next, then Brass Point 50m (160), Rough Brow 67m (216), Short Brow 66m (214), and the last Sister, just before Cuckmere Haven, is Haven Brow, the highest at 78m (253 feet).

8. Walk from Birling Gap over the Seven Sisters to Cuckmere Haven, about 3 miles. It is a further mile on to Exceat.

A lovely walk, it always feels more because of all the ups and downs. Dulcie Parkhurst says each season has its charm, but she would go when the flowers are at their best, the scent of thyme fills the air, and the song of the lark floats above.

Parts of the slopes are steep. Sheep and cattle often graze here so dogs must be on a lead, but also for their own sake; they can easily go over the cliff edge.

Looking west from Birling Gap to the Seven Sisters and Seaford Head

From the Birling Gap Hotel car park, turn inland and walk left at the back of the hotel along an unmade road between a few scattered houses. After the last house along the road there is a gate, through which a path veers right, past a wooded copse, leading to the South Downs Way on the left (with a bridle path ahead), and another gate opens onto the springy Downland turf. There are wide paths leading along the cliff top to the first of the Seven Sisters. Sections are sometimes fenced off to reduce wear by walkers. On the way up to the second Sister there is an obelisk recording that WA Robertson gave the land to the National Trust in memory of two brothers who died in the 1914-18 war.

This second Sister (Bailey's Brow) is higher, and ahead you can see the other Sisters and Seaford Head, a local nature reserve. Looking back, Belle Tout remains visible with the sheer cliff face below. In the afternoon sun rows of flints running horizontally stand out in the white perpendicular chalk cliffs. At high tide the Channel comes almost up to the base of all the cliffs, whereas at low tide shingle, sand and chalk is exposed as low shelves running out over a quarter of a mile into the Channel.

The third Sister, Flagstaff Point, has a seat and a Sarsen Stone (see Walk 9), with a broad path inland to Crowlink hamlet and Friston. Still visible are the Birling Gap coastguard cottages and, behind, Belle Tout. The dip which comes before the fourth Sister, Brass Point, used to be called Smugglers' Bottom, which had its own coastguard cottages. The turf slopes here can be quite steep, but what ideal spots to partake of lunch, with the pounding of the waves sounding almost as far away as the immobile telephone. The last three of the Sisters are higher, with the seventh, appropriately Haven Brow, the highest of all.

As you breast Haven Brow, the River Cuckmere lies before you, backed by the cliffs rising at Hope Gap to Seaford Head. Cuckmere Haven was once a busy estuary (possibly where King Alfred's ships sailed), it is now part of the Seven Sisters Park. This came into being in 1971 when the East Sussex County Council, with a grant from the Countryside Commission, bought the land to protect it from developers and enhance the ecological features. One can only trust that does not include reverting to caravan, or other theme, parks.

From the top of Haven Brow you drop down the chalk path to a man-made lagoon in the valley, which is a Mecca for ornithologists. The path can be slippery and there are often stretches of wear and tear by tourists. To avoid this path there is a track on the right turning inland which can be followed to pass the site of Exceat village, one of the casualties of the Black Death and French raids. Before 1347 over 100 people lived here, now the site of Exceat church is marked merely by a stone.[2] The valley path leads onto the beach, and turning right along the banks of the river brings you to a concrete road.

Both paths lead to Exceat Farm where the converted barns house the Exceat Farmhouse Restaurant, the Living World Natural History Exhibition, a Bike Hire Centre, and the Seven Sisters Centre which tells you all about the Seven Sisters Park. In the winter they are only open at week-ends, so check opening times.

The Revd AA Evans says that Edward Gorringe worked one of the last ox-teams at Exceat Farm in 1925. They were Welsh Blacks - formidable looking creatures, but gentle and amenable. At one time Friston Place had 16 draught oxen of Sussex breed. They were used in teams of six and although slower than horses, could work longer and they were cheaper to feed.[3]

From Exceat Farm there is a bus to Eastbourne. If you get off at East Dean you can walk along Gilbert's Drive back to Birling Gap.

Cuckmere Estuary

The little shingle beach at Cuckmere Haven is delightful with views back over the dazzlingly white Seven Sisters - an ever changing scene, for it is said that the cliffs were 200 feet further out to sea 100 years ago. From the beach you can follow the meanders of the old river or take a short cut along the "New Cut" made in 1844-46 at a cost of £900. Prior to 1844 the valley was in flood most winters.

Cuckmere Haven is full of history, from the lynchets showing evidence of ancient ploughing to smuggling in the 18th century, and being the only undeveloped natural harbour along the coast, it is the site for many films. During the 1939-45 war it was used as a decoy for Newhaven harbour. Inland it leads to Alfriston, a pretty Saxon village ("-ton" and "-ing" were Saxon word endings), and the 1220 Michelham Priory.

Cuckmere means fast flowing, inappropriate in the shallow and calm meanders, but suitable for all learners at the Cuckmere Valley Canoe Club. Seaford Head, complete with barrow, old fort and modern car park, is perhaps the best place to view the Seven Sisters. Looking east, from just above the old coastguard cottages, they look magical behind the river as it slips into the sea.

9. A walk from Friston to Crowlink and Flagstaff Point on the Seven Sisters cliffs and back again, not quite 3 miles.

This can be a diversion from Walk 8, otherwise drive up an unmade road from the A259, at Friston's Saxon church and pond, to the National Trust Crowlink car park. From here walk over the cattle grid and take either the made-up road towards the right which passes Crowlink hamlet to the sea, or take the high turf veering to the right, but more or less straight on past a copse of scrub, through a kissing gate that brings you along the top of the ridge, Flat Hill, to the Sarsen stone, at Flagstaff Point, where you can sit down. This is a magnificent viewpoint left to Birling Gap and the Belle Tout, to the right Cuckmere and Hope Cove in the distance, and the sea ahead. The Sarsen (means stranger) Stone was presented by Viscount Gage and erected in 1926 by the Society of Sussex Downsmen as a tribute to William Campbell - "...to whose munificent donation to the Seven Sisters Preservation Fund was largely due the purchase of the Crowlink Valley for the use and enjoyment of the nation".

To return take either of the ways back to the car park. Alternately turn left (ie. east) towards Birling Gap, but having reached a fence do not continue over the ladder stile, but turn left inland and walk bearing left keeping the scrubland to your right. If you notice a red-roofed barn keep it well on the right. Go over fields through two gates, cross the last field diagonally left and you will come back to Crowlink car park by the end house. Before you rejoin your car, look over the gate into the field on the right and take in the picture of the hollow in which nestles the hamlet of Crowlink, with views across to the sea. It is unspoilt Sussex.

APPENDIX 1

"Dew" ponds

These are hill ponds that hold water longer than those in the plains below. Some are of great antiquity, others were constructed in the last 100 years.

About 15 are found on the Beachy Head Downs. Two are near the road by Black Robin Farm, and another two behind Belle Tout, about 500m west of the Beachy Head Hotel.

Dew ponds were found in prehistoric and Palaeolithic ages down to Roman times. In chalk over 130m (400 ft) above the surrounding country no springs are likely to appear and, as puddled chalk is almost as good as clay to hold water, it was easier to trample out a pond than dig a well. Dew ponds were obviously important in Neolithic times for as Hubbard says, in an otherwise undistinguished book, they were carefully protected by ancient man.[1]

After Roman times there was a drift from the Downs towards the valleys of the Weald, but later as the Downs were used for sheep, dew ponds were revived. A few extant to-day have been going since the Middle Ages, with restoration every 20 years or so.

All consist of a circular depression, like a hollowed-out dish, with a chalk subsoil. They vary from 9-21m (30-70 ft) across and about 1-2m (3-6 ft) in depth at the centre. Most linings are clay, plus lime, straw and chalk. Another composite lining is mortar mixed with flints, layers of straw, hay and sometimes soot and lime with another layer of cement, or puddled clay. On the Downs puddled chalk is usual, although since about 1900 a concrete bottom is common, which lasts longer.

The gently sloping sides ensure a large area to receive as much rain as possible, for the main water supply is rain. The shallow sides encourage cooling at night and thus receive as much dew as possible. There is, however, only about 37mm (1.5 inches) of dew a year. Fogs and mists contribute water to the ponds, which have been shown to rise 50mm after fog, and as there is more mist on the Downs than in the valleys this source is more important than dew. Over a year, however, the amounts from condensation are minor compared with the amount from rain.

Dew ponds can dry out and once the bed dries it is liable to crack and allow any rain to run away into the chalk. If neglected, they cease to be waterproof once grasses and other plants grow through.[2]

Gilbert White refers to such ponds, but doesn't call them dew ponds and the term is not used before 1813. Even in 1877 HP Slade called them "artificial rain-ponds". Most people consider the term "Dew" pond is a twee Victorianism. Beckett said the shepherds called them "Sheep ponds".[3] Pugsley writes, "...Dew pond idea is one of the biggest pseudo-scientific swindles that has ever been foisted on unthinking readers."[4]

When in 1936 mains water was laid to the Downland farms, it also supplied the £1900 lavatories opened at Beachy Head in time for Whitsun.[5]

1. Hubbard AJ, Hubbard G. *Neolithic Dew Ponds & Cattleways.* Longmans Green, London 1907.
2. Martin EA. *Dew Ponds.* Werner Laurie, London.
3. Beckett A. *The Spirit of the Downs.* Methuen, London 1909.
4. Pugsley AJ. *Dew ponds in Fable & Fact.* Country Life 1938.
5. Fovargue HW. *Municipal Eastbourne 1883-1939.*

APPENDIX 2

Statistics for Beachy Head falls

There is a cliff whose high and bending head
Looks fearfully in the confined deep;
Bring me but to the very brim of it
..........................From that place
I shall no leading need.

Gloucester,   *King Lear IV. 1.*

It is seldom that brilliance does not have its reverse side and so with Beachy Head. Bold yet dangerous, and one of the country's best known tourist attractions, its fame is rivalled by its reputation for the loss of life by falling from the cliffs.

Only the Golden Gate Bridge in San Francisco approaches its total of lives claimed each year at an area of outstanding natural beauty. The windswept clifftop has proved to have an irresistible allure for people from all over the world who want to get off.

This section sets out the facts, figures and folklore for the falls at Beachy Head.

By legend there have been deaths on the cliffs since the 7th century. St Wilfrid was shipwrecked on the coast of the South Saxons and found them in the grip of a famine so severe that people were throwing themselves off the cliffs to escape its ravages and to leave food for those left behind. He taught the natives better methods of catching fish to help them through times of crop failure, and converted them to Christianity.[1]

Documentary evidence of deaths on the cliffs has existed for 400 years - in the Eastbourne Parish Register of 1600, there is an entry, "James Wykker that was slain by a fall from the cliff". More concrete evidence is the gravestone in Friston churchyard to Thomas Fletcher, Exciseman, thrown off the cliffs by smugglers in 1750; and thanks to modern technology we even have evidence of a July 1987 fall in full photographic colour.[2]

So there is little doubt that falls have occurred for many years: what numbers are we talking about?

Two or three deaths a year were reported in the 19th century. We know that during 1904-1911, when Chief Officer Hogben watched over, there were 13 deaths on the cliffs, increasing to about half-a-dozen a year by the middle of the century, with seven in 1959. Full details are impossible to obtain retrospectively, and the information is not always available, for example, during both World Wars not all the cases were reported.

For the quarter century, 1965 to 1989, full details of all deaths on Beachy Head are available - even though during this period there were minor alterations in verdict nomenclature, and in the extent of the police and coroner's districts. The total figures are given for five-year periods in Table 1 on page 126.

Recent rates remain much the same: in 1990 there were 26 deaths (the highest number in one calendar year), with 10 in 1991, 17 in 1992, and 19 in 1993, continuing the gradual increase in total numbers.

Who are these people, and are the falls accidents, suicides or murders?

Table 2 sets out the Beachy Head deaths by age and sex. There are about three men for every two women and the men tend to be younger, 62% under 45 years of age, compared with 49% of the women. Most women, 56%, were between 35 and 64.

In all cultures and activities sudden deaths in young men outnumber sudden deaths in women, so these figures alone do not help much in deciding whether the deaths are accidents, suicides or murders.

They would fit with a suicide picture, in that more men have always committed suicide than women (they are more violent, which includes violence against themselves, and they tend to choose more lethal methods - such as shooting, cutting and Beachy Head).

1. Deaths at Beachy Head over five year periods

	Total deaths over 5 years	Average per year
1965-69	20	4
1970-74	39	8
1975-79	65	13
1980-84	61	12
1985-89	65	13

The usual suicide ratio is 2:1, eg. for England and Wales in 1984 there were 2859 male suicide verdicts and 1456 female, with 1563 indeterminate deaths.[3] As jumping from a height is, however, more popular than other active methods among women (after the example of Sappho?), the Beachy Head ratio of 3:2 is compatible with suicides.

2. Beachy Head Deaths by age and sex 1965-89

	Age								
	5-14	15-24	25-34	35-44	45-54	55-64	65-74	75 and over	Total
Male	1	32	37	26	20	17	11	10	154
Female	0	8	19	20	18	16	12	3	96

Other information which might help the investigation could be changes in the domicile of victims, and in the sex ratio over the years, shown in Table 3.

This shows that, while the numbers fluctuate, over half come from outside East Sussex and there has been a gradual increase in male deaths, especially from outside the county - in other words they would have had to travel at least 20 miles, and in many cases much further. The last 30 years or so has coincided with many changes which might play a part: increased car ownership, greater TV coverage, newspaper circulation wars, feminism, the conversion to North Sea gas (which removed coal gas, a common method of suicide), and over the last ten years altered gun regulations, more unemployment, changes in the use of various drugs (barbiturates are used less to-day), and in the care of the mentally ill.

126

The obvious approach would be to accept the coroner's inquest verdicts. Any death on the cliffs would be referred for a coroner's inquisition, being a sudden death for which no doctor could certify the cause without further investigation.

3. Deaths at Beachy Head by domicile and sex over five year periods (excludes four with two addresses)

	Male			Female		
	Eastbourne	East Sussex	Outside ES	Eastbourne	East Sussex	Outside ES
1965-69	1	1	5	6	2	5
1970-74	4	0	15	6	3	8
1975-79	12	4	22	6	8	13
1980-84	12	11	16	4	12	6
1985-89	10	8	32	5	4	5

At first sight it seems clear from Table 4 that while suicide verdicts have increased, there are about equal numbers of suicides and other verdicts such as accidental and open.

A closer examination of the figures reveals that the proportions of suicide and open verdicts fluctuated wildly over the years. If we take the ten-year period 1965 to 1974 there were almost twice as many suicide verdicts as all other verdicts namely, 37 to 22, whereas in the five year period 1975-79 the ratio was reversed with only 21 suicide verdicts compared with 44 other verdicts, while for 1980-84 the numbers were about equal, 28 to 32, and in the last three years of the period there have been 34 suicides to 8 other verdicts.

It so happens that different coroners were in post for the periods mentioned. For a coroner to bring in a verdict of suicide he must be satisfied that intent was expressed, he cannot presume suicide. In the case of a Beachy Head death, "intent" is open to interpretation for there is no evidence, such as empty pill bottles, or tubing attached to an exhaust, and any notes or sounds could be blowing in the wind. It has been said that some coroners will only bring in a suicide verdict if there is physical proof of intent in the form of an unambiguous suicide note and this could be applied to John Dodd, the coroner from 1974-1980, whose main Beachy Head verdicts were over the years 1975 to 1979.

A fall in July 1975 demonstrates his approach. A 21-year-old Yorkshireman, who had received treatment for his mental condition, attempted suicide by throwing himself out of a window with only minor resultant injury, the next day he cut his wrist so deeply that he needed intensive therapy and a blood transfusion.

He was signed out of hospital, but the following day friends had to intervene to stop him throwing himself off a roof, and from drinking an overdose. The next day he and a friend went to Beachy Head (of all places), where he suddenly ran towards the edge and attempted to slide over until his friend grabbed his coat, when he said, 'If you don't let go I

127

will take you with me'. He struggled to free himself and eventually despite his companion's efforts the 21-year-old fell to his death. At the inquest the coroner commented, 'At no time on the cliff did he say he was going to take his life', and brought in an open verdict.[4]

4. Coroner's inquest verdicts at Beachy Head 1965-89

Year	Total	Suicide	Open	Other eg Misadventure, Accidental
1965	3	2	1	-
1966	6	5	1	-
1967	1	-	1	-
1968	5	4	1	-
1969	5	2	2	1
1970	4	4	-	-
1971	10	6	3	1
1972	6	2	2	2
1973	9	6	2	1
1974	10	6	3	1
1975	16	4	11	1
1976	9	1	8	-
1977	12	4	8	-
1978	11	4	7	-
1979	17	8	6	3
1980	5	3	2	-
1981	20	9	10	1
1982	9	3	6	-
1983	17	9	8	-
1984	10	4	6	-
1985	12	6	4	2
1986	11	8	2	1
1987	14	11	3	-
1988	12	10	1	1
1989	16	13	2	1
Total	250	134	100	16

Mr Dodd was not alone. On Easter Saturday 1981, a 19-year-old youth approached a photographer on the cliffs with the words, 'I hope you've got that loaded'. He walked off, turned on his heels 100m away, and at a run jumped over the edge, yelling as he went.[5] There was a history of depression, but as he had a blood alcohol of three times the legal driving limit, Mr EN Grace, the coroner, said he could have been confused and brought in an open verdict, which he was entitled to do.

Conversely, at an inquest in March 1989 there was a suicide verdict on an 81-year-old who had not left a note, had no psychiatric history and had not been seen to jump, but had placed a pile of clothes on the cliff. The coroner David Wadman said, 'One must take a practical view...he would not have made this journey for a scenic outing'. There was also a suicide verdict for a 38-year-old who jumped on 20 January 1990, Mr Wadman saying, 'It is true he did not leave a note and never indicated that he was minded to take his own life, but one has to take a realistic view'. This approach is reflected in the ratio of suicide to open verdicts over the last few years, although in 1997 deputy coroner, Alan Craze, returned an open verdict for a 25-year-old despite a history of depression, previous suicide attempts, exam stress, and a boyfriend and a sister who had committed suicide.

At Beachy Head, therefore, the coroner's verdicts are not necessarily indicative as to whether a death is a suicide.

Suicides, however, tend to have characteristic behaviour, no one element of which is conclusive, but taken together can be suggestive so that, unlike the coroner, a conclusion can be reached on the balance of probability.

General factors suggesting a suicidal death at Beachy Head are:- leaving a suicide note (all who left an unambiguous note had a suicide verdict); an act carried out in isolation with evidence of premeditation; previous suicide attempts (50% of suicides have made a previous attempt); a history of mental disorder; a patient in a psychiatric hospital; alcohol or drug problems; recent severe emotional upset; a male over 45 living alone; and a consultation with their doctor for a psychiatric condition in the previous three months.

The factors pertinent to Beachy Head which suggest suicide are:- being seen to jump or push off; a family history of suicide at Beachy Head; behaving strangely on the cliff edge (this includes bending over while stepping from one foot to the other, drinking alcohol at the edge, waving onlookers away, asking passers-by for a push off); individual factors such as taking a taxi directly to Beachy Head from a psychiatric hospital; and the leaving of possessions on the cliff top. This is a characteristic action of suicides. Dr EF Hoare, coroner in 1938, said, 'I have met many suicide cases in which the clothes have been left folded [on the cliff top]', and Dr AC Sommerville, another former coroner, once remarked, 'No woman just intent on a stroll along the cliff top would place her handbag down on the edge and go for a walk'.

A witness gives a graphic description of the last moments of a 40-year-old man from Stirling in 1966, 'I saw a man near the edge. He then walked back a short distance, divested himself of his coat and gloves, placed the clothes on top of each other, walked to the cliff edge and jumped immediately'.

No single factor, apart from a recent proven suicide note, is sufficient to confirm suicide, but whereas none of the accident verdicts had even three of these suicide factors, all the suicide verdicts had three or more, as did 97 of the 100 open verdicts, three of the seven misadventure and two of the three "other" verdicts. Some victims with open verdicts had eight suicide factors.

One fatality on the cliffs did not go to an inquest, death being considered due to illness, it is included in the "Other" category in Table 4, but there was a history of depression and suicide was likely. Another female, found in a crevice near the cliff top with injuries insufficient to cause death, probably died of exposure on a cold March night. Mr CS

Metcalfe, the deputy coroner, reasonably returned an open verdict, but she had a history of depression, was an in-patient at a psychiatric hospital and left possessions on the cliff top, so is considered a suicide.

It can therefore be presumed that 236 of the 250 deaths at the Beachy Head cliffs over the years 1965 to 1989 were suicides. Only seven holidaymakers (ie. those who had made holiday bookings) fell at Beachy Head (and five had a history of depression), and only two day-trippers fell, both of which were climbing accidents. In other words unless you are foolhardy and attempt to climb or sit on the extreme edge you should be safe at Beachy Head, keeping in mind that about a million people go there in the course of a year.

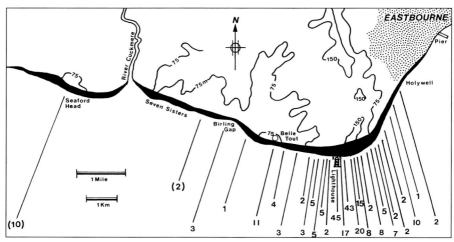

Site of falls at Beachy Head 1965-89. For seventeen falls it was not possible to delineate the site to within 100m. The falls in parenthesis are shown for completeness, but are not included in the Beachy Head figures

Visitors often ask, 'Where do the falls occur?' The site of falls is set out in the sketch map, which shows they occur all along the "Beachy Head" cliffs, but especially near the lighthouse - not attracted by the light, but by accessibility. It is within 100m of the road, and the other sites with ease of access (such as Belle Tout where the cliffs are about 10m from the road) also have an excess of numbers.

On the other hand, the Seven Sisters cliffs, which abut Beachy Head, have no easy car access road and very few deaths. The evidence is that most suicides jump within a few minutes of reaching the cliffs; people have been seen to dash out of a car, run straight to the edge and dive over, which is not possible at the Seven Sisters.

This could fit with the gradual increase in the number of male suicides who drive to Beachy Head from outside East Sussex, and who want a site accessible by car.

How are the falls distributed through the seasons? Table 5 gives the falls by calendar month and sex. More fall in the summer months, especially women (72% fell May/October) and this could again represent accessibility - there is a bus service to the top of Beachy Head in the summer. Proportionately most suicides in all countries are in the spring, yet strangely April is one of the months with the fewest suicides at Beachy Head.

130

For an active method of suicide women are well represented. Men often chose methods such as hanging, cutting and shooting (active methods), while women are more likely to use passive methods such as gassing or a drug overdose - although there is much overlap and availability is undoubtedly a factor.

Beachy Head may provide scope for both methods. Forty-three falls were witnessed in detail. Those described as "jumped over, stepped over, dived off, or ran over" are considered "active", and falls described as "slid over, lay down and rolled over, knelt down and bent backwards, and sat down and pushed off", as "passive". Active falls were witnessed for 19 men and eight women, passive falls for seven men and nine women.

As the males tended to be younger than the females, the average age of the "active" falls was about 40, compared with 56 for the "passive" falls, but the average age of both active and passive females was 55.

5. Deaths at Beachy Head by calendar month and sex, 1965-89

	Total	Male	Female
Jan	10	5	5
Feb	12	6	6
Mar	24	17	7
Apr	11	9	2
May	25	14	11
Jun	27	12	15
Jul	27	12	15
Aug	34	18	16
Sept	23	15	8
Oct	20	16	4
Nov	19	13	6
Dec	18	17	1

A multiplicity of views have been given as to why Beachy Head has this fatal attraction. Some say the ghost of a victim haunts the place, and one of the most contentious suggestions implies that the area has an evil presence which lures people to the edge.

In the 1950s a medium, Ray de Vakey, attempted to rid the cliff of its "macabre pull", and local white witch, Kevin Carlyon, speaks of an evil force that beckons weak-minded people to jump. Claims have been made that voices can be heard, similar to those of the Sirens in Greek mythology who tried to lure Ulysses and his sailors to their destruction.[6] The lashing of Ulysses to the mast was a more successful preventative move than for one Beachy

Head victim found bound with industrial tape, but when most of the suicides come from outside East Sussex (including the USA, Germany, France and Austria) and most jump as soon as they reach the spot, the Siren voices would need to be strident.

Victims are certainly lured to the spot, but by to-day's Sirens of publicity.

For a few victims Beachy Head has a special attraction ('I've always wanted Beachy Head', 'It's beautiful here and dangerous'), but as Dr Samuel Johnson said, 'Once a man has decided to end his life it matters not how'. Over 90% of those who fell had a psychiatric illness and many of the others had a recent emotional upset, and they are looking for a certain, lethal method, easily available (or accessible), which requires little or no preparation, and where they are unlikely to be interrupted. Most people know about Beachy Head's reputation, and the reporting of a recent suicide reinforces this knowledge.

In 1976 a 50-year-old man, in hospital following an overdose, was heard to remark after reading an article in the Brighton *Evening Argus* about Beachy Head deaths, 'Fancy putting that in the paper for people like me to see': a fortnight later he jumped. In 1987 a 26-year-old man (known by sight to Brian Lee, then licensee of the Beachy Head Hotel) was seen reading a newspaper. Later that day the man was found at the bottom of the cliffs and in his car was a copy of the *Sun* carrying a story about Beachy Head.

Barraclough has shown that reports of suicides in local newspapers do influence certain groups to commit suicide.[7]

It is not proven that radio or TV mentions affect the numbers making their way to Beachy Head, but suicides may increase after a suicide attempt on TV.[8] There have even been dramatic efforts to capitalise on the notoriety: for the film *Whoops Apocalypse* extras were hired to "jump off" Beachy Head.[9]

Arthur Beckett wrote in 1930, "Beachy Head has earned an unenviable notoriety as the scene of many suicides. In recent years these have occurred...annually and it is a strange fact that many of them occur in what may be described as sequences of two or three".[10]

An example of a sequence was seen in 1988. No deaths occurred on the cliffs in the first four months of 1988 until a 20-year-old TV star fell there in late April, to banner headlines. He had suffered from depression, had made a previous suicide attempt, had been in a psychiatric hospital, and there was a trail of cigarette butts leading to the cliff edge above where he was found. On this occasion Mr Wadman recorded an open verdict, 'Although it might appear that his death was self inflicted, I am not satisfied beyond reasonable doubt that this was the case'.[11] Even so, during the next four months ten further deaths on the cliffs occurred. As Seneca wrote, "...I have the refuge of death...".

There are innumerable examples of imitative suicides. An outbreak of suicides is said to have followed the death of statesman Robert Castlereagh in 1822, and similar bouts of suicides have accompanied even literary accounts, such as Goethe's *Werther* and Byron's *Manfred*. In the month of August 1962 there was a 75% increase in male suicides in Los Angeles after the death of Marilyn Munroe. Yet there was no increase in the rate for the year, substantiating the view that such events act as a spur for incipient suicides, but do not influence people who would not otherwise consider suicide.[12] More recently an epidemic of suicide by burning has been reported.[13]

Perhaps the most extensive imitative suicide epidemic occurred in Oshima, Japan in the 1930s. A schoolgirl jumped into a volcano in February 1933 and her death was featured widely. Over the following 18 months, 311 people killed themselves by jumping into the crater, including six on one day, until the government erected a barrier. The most Beachy Head has had, to June 1997, was three in a day, four times.

Such imitative actions have long been recognised. In 1841 the Registrar General wrote, "Some plan for discontinuing, by common consent, the detailed dramatic tales of suicide, murder and bloodshed in the newspapers is well worth the attention of their editors. No fact is better established in science than that suicide (and murder may perhaps be added) is often committed from imitation".[14]

The Eastbourne Medical Officer of Health wrote in 1906, "One cannot help remarking that if less notoriety were given to Beachy Head and similar suicides by the Press, weak-minded people would not so often think of suicide."[15]

The causes of suicide are more complex than Dr Willoughby proposed, but less publicity would deflect potential suicides away from the beauty spot.

As it is, many who go to Beachy Head intent on suicide do not carry out their threats, partly thanks to the many services on hand.

On average there are about two episodes a week when the police and coastguards are alerted because a note has been found or a known suicide risk was last seen heading for Beachy Head, or the hotelier has noticed someone behaving strangely. Most come to nothing, the individual having decided otherwise, or other agencies, such as the Samaritans, might have helped.

Dr Chris Chinery, of Hastings, tells of a patient who drove to Beachy Head in 1983, and, "...was actually heading for the edge when...two police cars raced in front of her".

In another example, Hubert Gregg, actor and theatre director, records that in 1955 he was under "almost intolerable strain" and drove to Eastbourne in the direction of Beachy Head. Finally he stopped his car and two policemen came over to help him.[16]

Police surgeon, Dr ZJ Ludwig of Bexhill-on-Sea, says that between May 1991 and May 1992 he saw about 30 suicidal cases who had intended to jump at Beachy Head and were brought instead to a place of safety by Eastbourne police.[17]

There is a group of suicides who visit Beachy Head more than once before finally jumping off. Some go two or three times in the course of a day, and others at an interval of a month or so.

How does Beachy Head compare with other sites in deaths from falling? In Britain it is the premier suicide spot, the next in line are the Severn Gorge with its Clifton suspension bridge, which had 127 falls over 20 years from 1973, and the Scarborough Valley bridge, said to have claimed 47 lives in 20 years. The cliffs at Dover, which are less accessible, have only one or two deaths a year on average, the cliffs at Torbay had 14 deaths during 1968-77, and Flamborough Head did not have one suicide between 1949 and 1976. There are occasional falls from Blackpool Tower[18] and blocks of flats, bridges, and multi-storey car parks, but no one place averages more than two or three deaths a year.

Overseas, there are falls from almost every natural and artificial edifice, including eight at one time from the top of a hotel at Salt Lake City in 1978. Many falls are recorded from the 985-foot Eiffel Tower (350 between 1889 and 1986[19], but said to be reduced since barriers were erected), the Notre Dame Cathedral in Paris, the 179-foot leaning Tower of Pisa (although only seven between 1940 and 1980) and, of course, the Golden Gate bridge at San Francisco.[20] The Golden Gate bridge, with a drop of almost 250 feet, had an average of over 15 deaths a year from 1937 to 1987, but since the side barriers were raised the number has fallen to less than at Beachy Head.

Round the world one thousand people commit suicide every day, one person every three hours in Britain, and in North America it is the third most frequent cause of death in the 15 to 44 age group. So the numbers involved are not insignificant, if only the figures could be believed, but there are inconsistencies between the nations of the world in every step of the reporting, investigating, ascertaining, adjudicating and recording of suicides. The number of suicides fluctuates slightly from place to place and year to year, but at any one time the official rate in one country could be 20 times that of another.

Mixtures of medical and legal systems exist. In Iceland, Australia and Bulgaria, the appointed officers must be legally qualified; in Norway, Poland and Yugoslavia (as in England and Wales) there are medical and legal officers.

The coroner is a peculiarly English figure. Other countries do not have a professional officer who investigates unexpected deaths. This is true of countries where the legal system is based on Roman law and in Islamic countries. The extent of any investigation also varies, for example some countries have an autopsy rate in such cases of less than 3%, and even Western Germany had an autopsy rate of only 40% compared with over 90% in England and Wales.

In Scandinavia presumption of suicide is not unusual. Suicide in Denmark is not of legal concern, there is no need for proof, and a kredslaeger's conclusion is reached on the balance of all probabilities, with the inevitable result that their suicide rate is about twice that of England and Wales.

Cultural differences play as much a part as procedure, with religious mores influential. In some countries insurance practices have an impact - if companies routinely do not pay out on a suicide verdict, juries tend to think more of the grieving widow and children than the validity of statistics. In other words any case with the slightest doubt will not have a suicide verdict returned. This is no recent change: comments on 15th century coroners' cases state, "Because of the stigma...suicides must have been cases [with]...no doubt".[21]

In Britain, until the Suicide Act of 1961, there was the added consideration that suicide was a felonious crime, although the verdict of *felo de se* (self harm) fell into disuse in the 1930s. Coroners brought in verdicts of suicide "while the balance of mind was disturbed" which avoided the punishment of a felony which involved forfeiture of life insurance policies and the right to a prayer book burial. Attempted suicide was also an offence, a misdemeanour, punishable by a fine or imprisonment.

Perhaps the rules for investigating violent deaths are not suited to provide the data required for a uniform classification. What is likely is that the figures for suicide world-wide are an underestimate. For some time doctors have expressed unease that if certain open, indeterminate or accidental verdicts are a manifestation of "not quite proven" suicides, such habits diminish the value of derived data for use as statistical tools. [22, 23]

As for murders at Beachy Head - even less easy to prove, a little push does not leave much evidence, and there are no fingerprints, or a knife or gun to exhibit. Over the period, 1965-89, three "unlawful killing" verdicts were recorded, for example, where a suicide has driven over carrying other people in the car with them, and three persons were found guilty of "attempted murder" at Beachy Head.[24]

Suicide pacts were seen at Beachy Head in 1979 and 1992. They remain a felony because of the danger of coercion, but in both instances there is little doubt that the participants were willing victims. Probably in the past murders have occurred, and stories of people being trussed up and tossed over in the Middle Ages abound. If it is difficult to prove to-day's suicides, the evidence for such murders is fragmentary at the least.

It is reasonable to conclude, therefore, that verdicts of accidental or suicidal death in England and Wales may be accepted, but that many open verdicts (and possibly a few misadventure or natural causes verdicts) cannot be accepted as the final arbiter, especially in circumstances such as Beachy Head. It is of interest that whilst appeals against an open verdict are most unusual, appeals against a coroner's verdict of suicide are not unknown.[25]

Any doubts about the reluctance of coroners to bring in a suicide verdict should be dispelled by the actions of Mr Robert Wilson, the East Berkshire coroner. At an inquest in February 1987, he said that he believed an 18-year-old youth (who fell from the top of a car park) had probably committed suicide, but after outlining the alternative verdicts he asked the family, 'Would you prefer it if I brought in an open verdict?' Even the father of the dead youth was surprised at the invitation. An open verdict was returned.[26]

An extreme example perhaps of some of the Beachy Head verdicts. Similarly, many of the Beachy Head cases are heartrending enough to feel for the family. Possibly the most poignant was an ex-Dr Barnardo's Homes orphan who had made a success of his life and decided to seek his natural family. He finally found his mother and a brother, but neither would speak to him. He jumped off Beachy Head, having removed all means of recognition, even cutting off the tabs from his clothes, so that it was two years before the police managed to identify him. Perhaps the two most unnecessary falls were the 18-year-old girl who stormed out of her house after being told not to "switch off" the electricity by tugging on the flex to pull out the plug, and was next found at Beachy Head, and the 21-year-old Cambridge first class honours graduate, who wrote that he didn't think he would be able to measure up to his own ambitions and he did not wish to become a mediocre scientist. The weirdest must be the family cases, such as the brother and sister who fell at Beachy Head some 13 years apart, and the death of a father and 70-year-old daughter separated by even more years. Perhaps the saddest was the 22-year-old pianist of international repute who died there in 1979 after buying a one-way rail ticket to Eastbourne. An accident in 1977 must run it close, when a 41-year-old Hove businessman parked his car on the top, about 50m from the edge, to have his lunch during which a thick mist came up. He was seen to start up his car and "drive steadily over the edge"; obviously he had lost his sense of direction.

What can be done to reduce falls at Beachy Head?

There will always be the occasional accident, and most present measures against suicides are largely ineffective. While changes in drug use (whatever the disadvantages of benzodiazepines they are mush less likely to be used for suicide than barbiturates) and intensive care units have saved the lives of many attempting suicide, no amount of psychiatric and social help materially affects the numbers, and although helplines may be useful in individual cases they do not reduce the incidence. Locally in 1957 there was a proposal to erect a 150-foot high cross at Beachy Head to deter would-be suicides, and a cliff top barrier is a recurrent suggestion, mainly from the national press.

Many depressives during an unworthiness phase will try any approach which is easily available and accessible, and hindering availability reduces the use of that method. In 1836 there was a suicide epidemic of jumping off the Monument in the City of London, which was stopped by a fence round the observation platform. In 1912 there were 3/million suicides from coal gas, which rose to 59/million in 1959 as more domestic gas appliances were installed. By 1975 lethal coal gas had been replaced by the safer North Sea gas, thus except for the relatively fewer deaths from engine exhausts, this suicide method disappeared, without much change in the suicide totals.

So a barrier to make the cliff edge inaccessible has to be considered, but a fence at Beachy Head would be a costly undertaking. It would be four miles long, and have to be replaced every other year or so to cope with erosion. It would also disturb the natural beauty; for a tall fence would be required - suicides have clambered over the metal one at Holywell, and elsewhere have climbed five-foot fences. There is, moreover, great doubt whether it would be effective, being a prey to the weather and vandalism over such a length. Reduction of publicity would deflect victims from Beachy Head to other methods, although some say more open discussion is preferred. There are several examples of suicide at Beachy Head after previous attempts elsewhere, and also of those who had been to Beachy Head, but finally chose another method. The real answer is improved and speedier-acting therapy for psychiatric illnesses, and ultimately their prevention.

What must not be forgotten is that Beachy Head is a place of outstanding natural beauty that is visited not just in safety, but with delight by millions of people every year.

It would also be surprising if there could be no lightening of the scene by the humorous moment. PC Brian Hinsbey recounts that he was called to Belle Tout with Inspector Clarence Jeffrey following a report that someone had gone over the cliff. They found a very distraught lady and the Inspector asked her to explain what had happened.

'I was standing near the edge', she said, 'And I called *Fido* to me, saying "Come on *Fido*, come on", and he came running up to me, went right by my legs and over the cliff. Are you going to see if my dear dog is all right?' 'Madam', replied Inspector Jeffrey, 'After that story I don't think you should be encouraging me to waste any more police time'.

Then there is the apocryphal story about the teetotal old lady who decided to jump, but thought she would imbibe a little Dutch courage beforehand. Having taken a swig of gin, the world didn't seem so bad and she went home instead.

1. Cook WV. *The Story of Sussex*. Combridges, Hove, 1920.
2. *The Sun* 28/7/1987.
3. OPCS Monitor DH4, 3/1985.
4. Brighton *Evening Argus* 25/7/1975.
5. *Eastbourne Gazette* 26/5/1981.
6. *Eastbourne Herald* 28/5/1988.
7. Barraclough BM, Shepherd D, Jennings C. Do newspaper reports of coroners' inquests incite people to commit suicide? *Brit J Psychiatry* 1977;13: 528-32.
8. Collins S. Health messages may have paradoxical effect. *BMJ* 1993; 306: 926.
9. *Eastbourne Post* 12/12/1985.
10. *Sussex County Magazine*. 1930; 1: 630.
11. *Eastbourne Herald* 30/4/1988, *Eastbourne News* 26/5/1988.
12. *Eastbourne Medical Gazette* 1980; 2: 137.
13. Ashton JR, Donnan SPB. Suicide by burning - a current epidemic. *BMJ* 1979; ii: 769-70.
14. Farr W. *Annual report of the Registrar General of Births, Marriages and Deaths in England*, 1841; III: 81-2. HMSO.
15. Willoughby WG. *Eastbourne MOH Report*, 1906; 66.
16. Gregg H. *Agatha Christie and all that Mousetrap*. William Kimber, London 1980.
17. Personal communication, 19/7/1992.
18. *Daily Telegraph* 25/10/1982.
19. *Ibid.* 29/11/1986.
20. Horton T. *Superspan: The Golden Gate Bridge*. Woolman, San Francisco 1983.
21. Hunnisett RF. *Sussex Coroners Inquests 1485-1558*. Sussex Record Society, Lewes 1985; 74.
22. Pounder DJ. Classifying suicide. *BMJ* 1992; 305: 472.
23. Surtees John. Classifying suicide. *BMJ* 1992; 305: 716.
24. *Eastbourne Herald* 2/4/1977. *Eastbourne Herald* 11/6/1977. *Daily Telegraph* 12/2/1981.
25. Surtees SJ. Suicide and accidental death at Beachy Head. *BMJ* 1982; 284:321-24.
26. *Daily Telegraph* 6/2/1987.

APPENDIX 3

Royal Sovereign (F1 20s 28M Horn (2) 30s)

The Royal Sovereign lightship first anchored over the shoal of that name in 1876, replacing a buoy (see Chapter 2). It is 7 sea miles from Eastbourne pier and 9 sea miles from the Beachy Head lighthouse.

In 1881 the crew was a mate, two lamplighters, and four seamen. Lifeboat rescues of injured crewmen were required in 1891 and 1948.

The last ship of the line, which took up position in 1954, was 137 feet long, and had a crew of a Master (Sam Sharman in the 1950s), two seamen, two fog signal operators and two lamplighters. Three anchors were available to keep it on station. The ship's light was of 600 000cp, one white flash every 20 seconds, the diaphone fog lamp sounded two blasts a minute, and latterly a radio beacon transmitted a warning signal night and day.[1]

Except for a break every three years to have its bottom scraped, this lightship remained in operation until superseded by a light-tower manned by three men.[2] It was towed away on 6 September 1971.

In 1966, Sir William Halcrow and Partners were commissioned by Trinity House to investigate the building of a telescopic concrete and steel light-tower, and later that year Christiani and Nielsen were awarded the contract. The tower was built near Newhaven between 1967 and 1969, and on 11/12 June 1970 the 4000-ton base was positioned and sunk in place, to be finally completed by the 1000-ton top on 16 May 1971. Its total height was 159 feet and the light had a range of 28 miles. The first principal keeper was Tom Whiston, and by usual lighthouse standards it was comfortable, each man having a room of his own.[3]

The final cost was £1.7m, almost double the estimate, the venture was dogged by bad weather and there were many delays, which put off Trinity House from repeating the exercise elsewhere, apart from changes in technology which were rendering lighthouses obsolete. [4, 5, 6, 7, 8]

At a cost of £180 000, but with the hope of saving £1.3m over 15 years, the light-tower was automated on 19 August 1994, and the light range reduced to 12 miles.[9, 10] Controlled from Harwich the optics are third order catadioptric, WF 20s 2 500 000cp. The horn is a 1000W Diaphone fog signal with fog detector, now two blasts every 30 seconds.[11]

1. *Eastbourne Gazette* 3/6/1959.
2. Beaver P. *A history of lighthouses.* Peter Davies,1971.
3. *The Times* 5/10/1985.
4. Brighton *Evening Argus* 17/5/1971.
5. *Eastbourne Gazette* 19/5/1971.
6. Brighton *Evening Argus* 18/6/1971.
7. *Daily Telegraph* 6/9/1971.
8. *Eastbourne Herald* 11/9/1971.
9. *Eastbourne Gazette* 22/12/1993.
10. *Ibid.* 17/8/1994.
11. Johnson D. *Lighthouses of England and Wales.* David & Charles, Newton Abbot 1975.

NOTES and REFERENCES

1. Beachy Head, Holywell to Birling Gap

1. Massingham HJ. *English Downland*. Batsford, London 1936.
2. Pugh P. *Grand Hotel*. Eastbourne 1987.
3. Sutcliffe S. *Martello Towers*. David & Charles, Newton Abbot 1972.
4. Hughes DE. *The Wish Tower Eastbourne*. Mirror, Eastbourne 1986.
5. Spears HD. *Local Martello Towers*. Crain, Eastbourne 1974.
6. Lower MA. *A History of Sussex*. John Russell Smith, London 1870.
7. Parry JD. *The Coast of Sussex*. Longman 1833.
8. Hope Moncrieff AR. *Guide to Sussex*. A&C Black 1911.
9. Meynell E. *Sussex*. Robert Hale, London 1947.
10. Holgate R. *Neolithic site and Napoleonic camp*. Sussex Archaeological Collections (1988); **126:** 21.
11. *Eastbourne Advertiser* 1/12/1994.
12. *Eastbourne Herald* 17/12/1994.
13. W Camden. *Britannia* 1607 ed. trans. R. Gough. 1806, p 271.
14. Lucas EV. *Highways & Byways in Sussex*. Macmillan, London 1924. Hannah IC. *The Sussex Coast*. Fisher Unwin, London 1912.
15. Brabant FG. *Rambles in Sussex*. Methuen, London 1909.
16. *Eastbourne Herald* 25/1/1986.
17. Milton J. *Some notes on sport in Eastbourne*. ELHS NL 1988; **70:** 18-24.
18. *Sussex County Magazine* 1938; **XII:** 571.
19. *Eastbourne Medical Gazette* 1978; **2:** 72.
20. Coates R. *Belle Tout, note on name*. SAC 1979; **117:** 264.
21. Bradley RJ. *Iron-age fort at Belle Tout*. SAC 1971; **109:** 8.
22. Bradley RJ. *Chalk-cut shaft at Belle Tout*. SAC 1974; **112:** 156.
23. Drewett PL. *Iron-age fort at Belle Tout*. SAC 1975; **113:** 184.
24. Stevens L. *Chalk-cut shaft at Belle Tout*. SAC 1979; **117:** 260.
25. Holgate R. *Erosion of Belle Tout*. SAC 1986; **124:** 243.
26. *Sussex County Magazine* 1939; **XIII:** 406.
27. *Eastbourne Herald* 18/10/86.
28. *Sussex County Magazine* 1932; **VI:** 798.
29. Reed T. *The Fishermen and Boatmen of Eastbourne*. ELHS Crain, Eastbourne.
30. Thomas A. *Fields of Mystery*. SB, Seaford 1996.

2. Lights and lighthouses, beacons and bonfires

1. *Sussex County Magazine* 1932; **V1:** 565.
2. Hughes PM. *The Seven Sisters, a guide to East Dean and Friston*. Sussex Ptrs, Eastbourne.
3. *Sussex County Magazine* 1928; **II:** 21.
4. *Ibid*. 1936; **X:** 469.
5. Gilbert R. *Shipwrecks, Cuckmere Haven to Langney Point*. ELHS 1988 p 26.
6. *Eastbourne Gazette* 23/2/1876, 1/3/1876.
7. *Eastbourne & District Advertiser* 4/4/1985.
8. *Ibid*. 18/6/1980.
9. *Daily Telegraph* 24/6/1983.
10. *Eastbourne Herald* 24/12/1982.
11. Armstrong R. *The Beachy Head Light*. Mirror, Eastbourne.
12. Kitchen F. *Fire Beacons in Sussex*. SAC 1986; **124:** 179.
13. *Eastbourne Gazette* 8/6/1977.
14. *Eastbourne Herald* 11/6/1988.

3. Shipwrecks and Lifeboats

1. Hilaire Belloc in Wilfrid Ball's book *Sussex* describes the dangers of sailing round Beachy Head, "Each puff of wind comes from a different direction".
2. Gilbert R. *Shipwrecks, Cuckmere Haven to Langney Point*. ELHS 1988.
3. *Sussex Weekly Advertiser* 4/1/1796. RM Caldecott built a folly on Beachy Head in the 19th century.
4. Budgen W. *Old Eastbourne*. Sherlock, London 1912.
5. *Sussex County Magazine* 1926-7; **I:** 212-218.
6. *Ibid*. 1934; **VIII:** 445.
7. *Lewes Advertiser* 5/4/1779.
8. *Sussex Weekly Advertiser* 10/3/1788.

9. *Ibid.* 26/1/1789 & 1/2/1789.
10. *Ibid.* 16/5/1796.
11. Royer J. *East Bourn, a descriptive account of the village.* 2nd Ed. 1799.
12. Hodsoll V. *Apparatus for saving shipwrecked mariners preserved at Mr Willard's Farm.* ELHS NL 1990; **78:** 8-11.
13. *Sussex County Magazine* 1935; **IX:** 361.
14. Morris J, Hendy D. *The Story of the Eastbourne Lifeboats.* 1981.
15. *Eastbourne Gazette.* 27/1/1875.
16. *Ibid.* 12/4/1876.
17. Towner Art Gallery and Local Museum, Accession no. 1488.
18. *Sussex County Magazine* 1939; **XIII:** 377.
19. *Eastbourne Gazette* 18/5/1904.
20. The *Priscilla Macbean* was returned to Eastbourne by her last owner and the hulk is on Eastbourne beach.
21. *Eastbourne Herald* 29/2/1936. *Eastbourne Gazette* 4/3, 18/3, 25/3/1936.
22. *Eastbourne Gazette* 28/10/1968.
23. *Daily Telegraph* 25/2/1976. *Eastbourne Herald* 28/2/1976.
24. *Eastbourne Herald* 18/11/1989.
25. *Ibid.* 4/1/1997.

4. Coastguards, Signals and Smuggling

1. *Sussex County Magazine* 1935; **IX:** 362. (To avoid confusion, another ship named *Juno* sank off Beachy Head after a collision in March 1881.)
2. *The 1841 Census for Eastbourne.* ELHS 1990.
3. Hope-Moncrieff AR. *Guide to Sussex* A&C Black 1911.
4. *East Dean Village Walk,* Micheldene WI 1980.
5. Milton FR. *The Signal Post Watch Tower and Guns of Beachy Head.* ELHS NL 1991; **79:** 12-18.
6. Lewis M. *The Admiralty Semaphore Station at Beachy Head.* ELHS NL 1988; **70:** 15-16.
7. *Sussex County Magazine* 1938; **XII:** 607.
8. Sharpin IM, Williams CF. *A Postal History of Eastbourne.* Christians, Eastbourne 1972.
9. Suggested books; Douch J. *Smuggling.* Crabwell 1985. Milton FR. *The Fight against Smuggling around Eastbourne and Newhaven.* Family Roots, Eastbourne 1991. Webb W. *Coastguard.* HMSO 1976. Waugh M. *Smuggling in Kent and Sussex.* Countryside, Newbury 1985.
10. Lucas EV. *Highways & Byways in Sussex* Macmillan, London, 1924.
11. Cook WV. *The Story of Sussex.* Combridges, Hove 1920.
12. *Daily Telegraph.* 22/3/1992.
13. *Eastbourne Chronicle* 8/6/1951.
14. *The Guardian* 29/11/1994.

5. Cliff Rescues and Recoveries

1. *Eastbourne Herald* 17/5/1980.
2. *Eastbourne Gazette* 2/9/1987.
3. *Ibid.* 8/8/1987.
4. *Eastbourne Gazette* 18/11/1981. *Eastbourne Eagle* 20/5/1982. *Eastbourne Herald* 22/5/1982.
5. *Eastbourne Herald* 2/2/1985.
6. The *Gwalia* was owned by WL Wyllie, the maritime painter. She started life as a barge, the *New Zealand,* and renamed *Four Brothers* until converted into a yacht.
7. Hughes PM. *East Dean with Friston Parish Magazine* 10/1960, 2/1961.
8. *Eastbourne Gazette* 31/7/1974.
9. *Ibid.* 9/4/1980.
10. *Ibid.* 11/10/1978.
11. *Ibid.* 26/4/1978.
12. *Eastbourne Gazette* 9/4/1980. *Eastbourne Herald* 12/4/1980.
13. *Eastbourne Gazette* 30/1/1980.
14. *Ibid.* 22/1/1983.
15. *Ibid.* 5/2/1983.
16. *Ibid.* 4/8/1976.
17. *Eastbourne Herald* 18/8/1979.
18. *Eastbourne Post* 10/10/1985.
19. *Eastbourne Citizen* 7/6/1990.
20. *Eastbourne Herald* 9/4/1994.
21. *Eastbourne Gazette* 4/7/1979.
22. *Eastbourne Herald* 29/3/1980.

23. *Eastbourne Gazette* 25/6/1980.
24. *Eastbourne Herald* 11/2/1978.

6. Climbing
1. Haskett Smith WP. *Rock Climbing in the British Isles - England.* Longmans Green. 1894.
2. *Daily Telegraph* 29/6/1986.
3. Chambers GF. *Eastbourne Memories.* Sumfield, Eastbourne 1910.
4. Pyatt EC. *Climbing and Walking in South East England,* David & Charles, Newton Abbot, 1970.
5. Bullock HS. Chalk Climbing on Beachy Head. *Climbers' Club Journal.* February 1899; 91-97.
6. Crowley EA. Chalk Climbing on Beachy Head. *Scottish Mountaineering Club Journal.* May 1895.
7. *Sussex County Magazine* 1935; **IX:** 688.
8. *Eastbourne Gazette* 1/8/1979. *Eastbourne Herald* 18/8/1979.
9. *Eastbourne Herald* 13/6/1981.
10. *Sussex County Magazine* 1936; **X:** 562. *Ibid.* 1937; **X1:** 557. *Ibid.* 1938; **XII:** 485.
11. *Sussex Life* 1971; **7:** 91.
12. *Daily Mail* 8/4/1980.

7. Lucky Escapes
1. *Eastbourne Gazette* 14/3/1979.
2. *Eastbourne Herald* 10/7/1976.
3. *Daily Telegraph* 3/5/1976. *Eastbourne Gazette* 5/5/76.
4. *Eastbourne Herald* 29/7/1978. *Eastbourne Herald* 30/12/1978. *Daily Mail* 16/4/1980.
5. Brighton *Evening Argus* 26/6/1979. *Eastbourne Herald* 30/6/1979.
6. *Eastbourne Gazette* 18/7/1979. *Sunday Mirror* 23/9/1979.
7. *Eastbourne Eagle* 4/2/1982. *Daily Telegraph* 31/1/1982 & 1/2/1982.
8. *Eastbourne Herald* 27/11/1982.
9. *Eastbourne Gazette* 5/8/1987. *Eastbourne News* 6/8/1987.
10. Brighton *Evening Argus* 5/3/1988. *Eastbourne Herald* 5/3/1988.
11. *Eastbourne Herald* 29/6/1985.
12. *Eastbourne Gazette* 23/2/1977.
13. *Eastbourne Herald* 1/3/1980.
14. *Eastbourne Gazette* 16/7/1980.
15. *Daily Telegrap*h 12/2/1981.

8. Beachy Head goes to War
1. Cook WV. *The Story of Sussex.* Combridges, Hove 1920.
2. Stevens L. *The Battle of Beachy Head.* ELHS Newsletter 1990; **77:** 13-15.
3. Beckett A. *The Battle of Beachy Head.* Sussex County Magazine 1929; **III:** 378.
4. Sanderson M. S*ea Battles.* David & Charles. 1975; 31-32.
5. Thornton N. *Sussex Shipwrecks.* Countryside Books. 1988; 100-113.
6. Mordal J. *Twenty five centuries of Sea Warfare.* London Abbey Library 1959.
7. *Sussex County Magazine* 1929; **III:** 812.
8. Bourdillion FW. *Beachy Head.* Paper read before the Eastbourne Natural History Society 1884.
9. Gilbert R. *Eastbourne prepares to meet Old Boney.* Crain Eastbourne.
10. A *Mendi* was torpedoed in mid Channel during a snowstorm in February 1917 with the loss of 800 lives.
11. *Sussex County Magazine* 1932; **VI:** 360.
12. Surtees John. *The Princess Alice and other Eastbourne hospitals.* ELHS 1994.
13. Worsfold E. *Friston Pond.* 1990.
14. Ockenden M. *Eastbourne Herald* 19/8/1989. Humphrey G. *Wartime Eastbourne* Beckett 1989.
15. Burns MG. *Bader, the Man and his Men.* Arms & Armour Press (Cassell), London 1990.
16. Longstaff-Tyrrell P. *Eastbourne Local Historian* ELHS 1997; **103:** 8.
17. *Eastbourne Medical Gazette* 1978; **2:** 95. Elliston RA. *Lewes at War 1939-45* Alma Cott 1995.
18. Donald Sinden, the actor, in a Southern TV program, 29/6/1980, explained the ENSA grading of shows. 'Grade A shows went to Aldershot and a D show to an Ack-Ack site at Beachy Head'.
19. Donne J. *Eastbourne Herald* 15/12/1979, 22/12/1979, 29/12/79.
20. *Eastbourne & District Advertiser* 29/1/1987. Nesbit R. *Aeroplane Monthly.* Feb. 1987.
21. *Eastbourne Herald* 11/6/1988.
22. *Ibid.* 15/8/1987.
23. *Eastbourne & District Advertiser* 15/4/1987. *Eastbourne Herald* 25/4/1987.

9. Natural History
1. Lower MA. *A History of Sussex.* John Russell Smith, 1870.

2. *A Natural History of the Eastbourne Area,* ed. Munson DE. ENH&AS 1981.
3. Hannah IC. *The Sussex Coast.* Fisher Unwin, 1912.
4. Farrant J. ELHS NL 1987; **66:** 12, quoting Macky J. *A Journey Through England.* 1713.
5. *Sussex County Magazine.* 1932; **VI:** 77.
6. *Ibid.* 1935; **IX:** 129.
7. Beckett A. *The Wonderful Weald.* Methuen London 1924 (first published by Mills & Boon).
8. *Sussex County Magazine* 1935; **IX:** 54.
9. *Ibid.* 1935; **IX:** 56.
10. *Ibid.* 1935; **IX:** 389.
11. White G. *The Natural History of Selborne.* 1788 (Penguin Ed. 1977).
12. *Sussex County Magazine* 1939; **XIII:** 780.

10. Walks around Beachy Head and the Seven Sisters

1. Drewett PL. *Archaeology of Bullock Down.* SAC Monograph 1982.
2. Unlike Beachy Head, the Domesday Book had a mention of Exceat. *Domesday Book Sussex,* ed. Morris J. Phillimore, Chichester 1976.
3. Wills in *Bypaths in Downland,* Methuen, 1927, describes seeing the oxen being worked by stockman, WE Wooler. The pairs had picturesque names.

ACKNOWLEDGEMENTS

To my wife, Sheila, and CD Backhurst, Dr SK Bangert, Phil Bell, Central Records Office, Lewes, Sarah Clarke, Terry Connolly, A Craze, Petra Dalton, M Davey, J Dodd, Becky Dunne, Eastbourne Borough Council - Tourism & Community Services (Marianne Frith, Gill Kirkman), Eastbourne Central Library, Eastbourne Postgraduate Medical Centre (Liz Oliver-Taylor), Annemarie Field, Nicolette Fox, Dr DJ Gooding, EN Grace, Vida Herbison, Vera Hodsoll, Imperial War Museum, Heath Jeffries, Chris Johnson, Lord Chamberlain's Office, Justin Lycett, Lou McMahon, David Manners, CS Metcalfe, Rosemary and John Milton, Frances Muncey, Dr JD O'Connor, Michael Partridge, Royal Mail Stamps Marketing, Garry and Rosemary Russell, AP Watt Ltd on behalf of the National Trust (for the Kipling extract), Dr AC Sommerville, Lawrence and Pat Stevens, GE Stickler, Nick Taylor, Dr C Tourle, Towner Art Gallery & Local Museum (Fiona Robertson, Jerry Bird, Sarah Blessington, Norman Culshaw, Miles Comfort, Mary Elliott, Emma Olivari, Colin Napier, Anne Russell, Catherine Tonge), Trinity House, Phil Wade, D Wadman, and many others.

The original coastguard auxiliaries who assisted Garry Russell in 1973 were Bob Andrews, John Clark, Paul Gregory, Barry Lee, Ted Lee, Derek Morley, Harry Morley, Freddie Sherwood, and Paul Wells.

The front cover is of Beachy Head and lighthouse from the west, the back cover an afternoon view from the east, both photographs by Nick Taylor.

The end of the line for steam locomotive No. 32424: the name plate is now in the Towner Art Gallery and Local Museum, Eastbourne

INDEX